Breaking Free
And Staying Calm

DEBRA LINDSEY

Copyright © 2025 *Debra Lindsey*

All rights reserved.

ISBN: 978-1-80623-924-5

DEDICATION

For my loving parents Norma & Dave, who saved me from myself.
For my siblings, Andrew, and Lesley, who were my pillar of strength.
For my children Tamara and Ben, who are my world.
For my husband Dean, who is my missing jigsaw piece.

But most of all I owe myself the biggest apology for
putting up with what I didn't deserve

CONTENTS

ACKNOWLEDGMENTS vi

1 THE GIRL BORN BY SURPRISE 1

2 SWIMMING POOLS AND MULBERRY TREES 10

3 ALL CREATURES: BIG AND SMALL 20

4 FAMILY AND FRIENDS 30

5 SHADOWS IN THE SUNLIGHT 34

6 UNPREDICTABLE TIMES AHEAD 41

7 A NEW FLAG, A NEW FUTURE 47

8 A WOLF IN SHEEP'S CLOTHING 59

9 TOXIC ISOLATION AND WALKING ON EGGSHELLS 66

10 WELCOMING BABY TAMARA 78

11 A LIFELINE WITH EMPTY PROMISES 89

12 THE END AND NEW BEGINNINGS 97

You matter.
Read that again...

ACKNOWLEDGMENTS

I want to say thank you to the rare few individuals in my life who have

- ♥ listened without judgement,
  - ♥ spoken without prejudice,
    - ♥ helped me without entitlement,
      - ♥ understood without pretension
        - ♥ and loved me without conditions

1
THE GIRL BORN BY SURPRISE
A Spark in the Middle of the Night

It was five minutes past midnight on the 17th of August, 1970, when I entered the world—not only unexpectedly early, but on my maternal grandfather Norman's birthday. A perfect and poetic beginning, they say. I like to think I was giving him the best birthday gift he had ever received.

Born in Salisbury, Rhodesia (now Harare, Zimbabwe), in August, I burst into the world with a loud wail at the Lady Chancellor Hospital. My dad, David, had dropped Mum Norma off at the maternity unit and, after getting her settled, continued on to work, expecting Mum to be induced later the next day. After all the heartbreak of losing previous pregnancies through miscarriage, they were taking no chances. Mum's Rhesus -ve blood group had caused the issue of not allowing the babies to stick to her womb and grow, so they had just come away after a couple of months.

Eventually, after the 8th loss, she agreed to have a procedure called the Shirodkar Suture, which is a cervical cerclage technique used to support the cervix during pregnancy, particularly in cases of cervical insufficiency - it holds the baby in to allow the fetus to grow and be nurtured naturally. Once the stitch is removed, the baby can be born naturally.

Mum's stitch was removed later that evening; however, I had other plans. I was in a hurry. An hour later, a nurse phoned Dad to tell him he had a little baby daughter, and in utter disbelief, he told her she must have the wrong man—his wife wasn't due until later the next day. But no, I had made my entrance at 00:05 am on the 17th, ready to make my mark on the world. And I have done just that.

I was born into a family bursting with love and laughter. My parents, Norma and David, were devoted to one another, united in purpose and gentle in strength. Mum was affectionately known as Weff, a nickname given to her by Dad. They raised my siblings and me with a mixture of affection, firm discipline, and values that have shaped me to this day. Respect, kindness, and loyalty were not taught—they were lived, every single day.

Dad, born in Leicestershire, England, was a strong and muscular Englishman with tanned arms and legs from the African sun, upright and confident.

Weff was a tall and beautiful English lass, born in Nottingham, England, with a mop of soft, wavy curls and a bright smile on her face, always with arms ready to embrace you.

Only two weeks after being married in a gorgeous ceremony in Leicestershire, England, Dad embarked on a journey with his beautiful bride to the other side of the world, to re-join his parents, Win & Leslie Torry and his two younger sisters, Ann & Margaret, in the expansive, dusty, hot, baked, arid but beautiful Rhodesia. Grandad Leslie was a Warrant Officer in the Royal Air Force and had been posted out there in WW2 from England.

My siblings, my older brother Andrew, five years ahead of me in mischief and wit, and my little sister Lesley, born nine years after me and so tiny when she arrived that she fit into the palm of Dad's hand—a 2lb miracle. While Andrew was the sharp-witted mastermind, always a step ahead and knee-deep in trouble, I was the tomboy: berry-brown face, scraped-kneed, climbing trees and diving into the pool before I could barely walk. I was always trying to keep up with Andrew in his shadow, being the annoying little sister trying to copy him and play with him and his friends. Lesley was the delicate balance to my chaos—a playful, sweet child who gave me my first real lessons in nurturing. I dressed her up like a doll and played mum, under the watchful eye of our own.

My earliest lessons in creativity came from those around me. While Andrew excelled in academics and Lesley was the sporty one, I found my joy in expression—drawing, painting, and later in life elaborate wedding and birthday cakes. I lived for colour and imagination, and the encouragement from my parents never wavered.

We lived on a beautiful five-acre plot, side by side with my paternal grandparents, Grandma Win and Grandad Leslie, who lived next door to us. We were a close-knit family—grandparents, parents, children, and extended relatives—interwoven by shared meals, our regular 10 am tea time at Grandma's and then the stroll over to ours for 3 pm tea time, warm afternoons, and the kind of support that made you feel like you could face the world.

Because the property was so vast, Weff & Dad hired help in the form of Matthew, our houseboy, and John, our garden boy.

Well catered for, they had their own quarters (khaya) on the property away from the main house, and the job came with a salary and a Christmas bonus. Matthew was a piccanin (young boy) when he started helping Weff in the house. Over the years, he grew with our family, and eventually he got married himself, and Matthew and his wife Margaret had their own family and continued to work for us.

I often used to "visit Matthew and Margaret" at their khaya at the end of the garden to play with their children. They would invite me to sit with them around their fire, sharing their sadza (stiff savoury porridge), nyama (meat & gravy) & rape (kale). They'd teach me some of their ways and customs, showing me how to roll little balls of sadza, making a deep dent with your thumb in order to dip and scoop from the communal nyama pot bubbling over the fire, whilst his little children would giggle shyly at my fumbling. A dish of warm water was prepared, ready to wash your hands first, and only with your right hand (it is customary to show respect for your host or hostess; the right hand is always used to eat with).

Matthew was originally from Mozambique, and when we moved across town, they moved with us to continue working with our family. John didn't, and we never saw him again.

Our family tea times were notable in terms of signalling tools down, time to take a break. The tea-trolley would be prepared by Grandma's house girl with clean cups & saucers and a large pot of tea under a tea cosy sewn in the shape of a house. Grandad Leslie would stew the Tanganda tea leaves in the teapot, pouring the hot steaming liquid into the tea cups, straining, and saving the tea leaves for Grandma to compost the garden, whilst Grandma passed around the biscuit tin. Always gingers, custard cremes or iced zoo biscuits used to be hiding in there, with the occasional chocolate digestive or two. Grandad Leslie made the best tea in the world, always handing me my "special plastic yellow glitter beaker" with the sweet milky tea. Unlike my other Grandad Norman, who loved his tea the stronger the better - "you can stand the spoon up in that" we would joke.

Grandma & Grandad's 10 am teatime always took place on their long veranda with the overstuffed comfy chairs covered in blankets, overlooking their front lawn. There was a little red leather bucket chair at one end where Spot the dog used to curl up and sleep. There was a chalkboard up on the wall to one side, with a little stool for me to climb up and draw pictures of stick men and flowers. Andrew always beat me at noughts and crosses and hangman—games he took too seriously with his 5-year-old sister— but he had to win every time. I didn't care; I was just glad he wasn't teasing me for a bit. There were always half-drawn pictures smudged with chalk dust as if the little artist had left in a hurry to some other activity going on. We'd sit on the walls sipping tea or drinking Mazoe orange squash whilst the adults chatted about the day's chores ahead or about politics.

3 pm tea time was similar but different. Afternoon tea was over at our house. I used to run halfway between Grandma & Grandad's and our hedge to see if they had started walking over yet. As soon as I spotted them, I'd run over to Grandma and hold her hand, willing her to walk faster to ours. By the time we got to our veranda, Weff had already prepared her tea trolley with a lacy teacloth under brown stoneware teacups and saucers, a large matching teapot, milk jug and sugar bowl with a crocheted lid. Usually there would be scones or flapjacks, and always the favourite biscuits.

I would usually be in my swimming costume, either dripping wet from an after-lunch swim, or I'd be glowing warm brown, having already dried out from my swim, but always ready to jump back in.

"Grandma, graaanndmaaa, Wee-eff, Daddy, Grandad.... look what I can do..." I would yell from the top of the pool slide. I would be lying backwards and upside down, about to fly down the slide in a backwards dive headfirst. I am sure I must have given Weff several frights; instead she looked on, shading her eyes from the sun and applauding my latest trick.

There was always laughter in our house. Like the time Andrew convinced our gardener that if he buried his wages in the garden, a money tree would grow. The poor man, trusting and hopeful, did as Andrew said—only for Andrew to dig it up and run off with it as soon as he turned his back. He got properly reprimanded, the gardener was made whole, and the story lives on in family lore as a glimpse into the entrepreneurial mind of my big brother.

Of course, I got into trouble, too. I always wanted to keep up with Andrew, which meant getting into scrapes of my own. Weff—quick, determined, and wielding a wooden spoon—chased me more than once around the mulberry trees. But I had a trick: I would jump into the pool and swim to the middle, knowing full well she couldn't swim and wouldn't follow me in.

"You've got to come inside sometime!" she would shout, shaking her spoon. We would both laugh about it later.

Although I would love to claim Weff all to myself, she wasn't only Mum to Andrew, Lesley and me. She was Mum to all our cousins and neighbourhood friends.

So many times, I'd hear "Aunty Norma, can I come over and play?" with never a "no" to be heard. She was the go-to person who would get you out of trouble, whilst a little face would be hiding behind her skirt.

When the baker boy used to knock on the door with his basket of bread, she would lift me up to stand on the wheel of his cart to sneak a cream doughnut.

When the Lyons Maid or Dairy Board ice cream boys used to cycle their ice cream carts in the streets, selling their icy treats, she was always ready with some coins for us to run out and choose a lolly or ice cream.

I used to listen out for "Couscous, the veggie man" too, announcing his arrival with the sound of his bicycle bell. He would ride up to our back door, his wicker basket overflowing with fresh vegetables, and Weff would choose what she wanted. She would always give me the money to pay him, making me feel so important. He would then cycle next door to Grandma's to do the same.

Very often, a singsong calling in the street would make us aware that the Mielie Maid was on her rounds. This was a native woman carrying a big silver tin bath on her head, full of mielies (fresh corn on the cob) picked from the fields. She would shout in her shrill call, "Mieeeeeee-lieeeeees", and if prepared and cooked properly, they were utterly delicious. Often, Weff would be boiling mielies in a big pot until tender and soft and slathered in butter, salt, and pepper for us to gobble down with the butter running down our chins.

Weff was the queen of our birthday parties. Always a bunch of cousins and friends would enjoy a range of party food on the birthday table with the spectacular birthday cake in the centre of it, party games always included "pass the parcel" with a gift wrapped multiple times in coloured wrapping paper. She would hide sweets in the trees in the orchard and arrange sack races or three-legged races, leaving us out of breath, laughing and rolling on the grass. The Jacaranda trees would bloom purple above us, and life was just... Full. Rich. Warm.

Grandad Leslie was a mechanical genius with always something up his sleeve. He excelled himself when he built a contraption we called the Sandyacht: a kind of home-made joyride on fat wheels that could carry a dozen children around the garden.

I was raised on love and laughter, creativity and consequence, freedom, and protection. I was also raised on uncertainty and unspoken fear. But that came later.

In the beginning, there was colour and light and warmth. And through everything that followed—fear, loss, chaos, danger—this is what I carried with me: the sense that I belonged to something strong. That I was safe in the world, even if only in memory. That I had been born on a special day, into a family that knew how to love.

I was a girl born by surprise.

A spark in the middle of the night.

A surprise. A gift.

And that spark has never gone out.

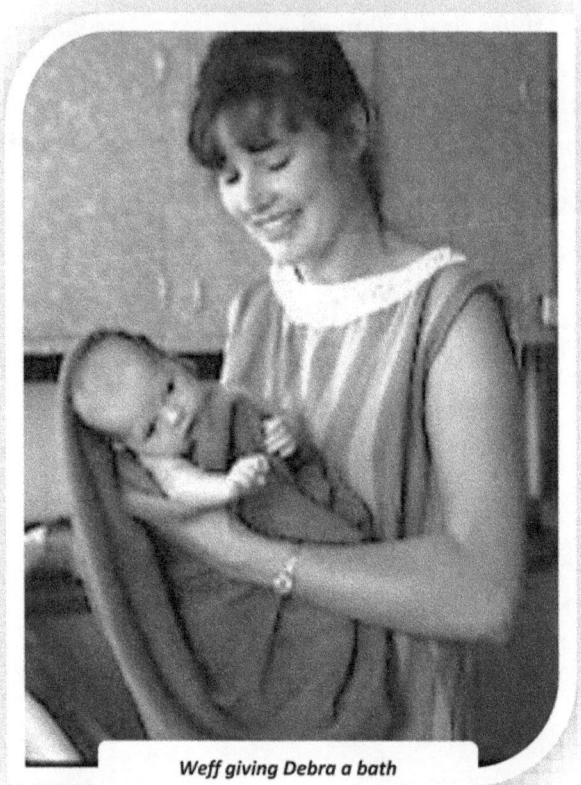
Weff giving Debra a bath

Debra (2) at a birthday party

Grandad Leslie (centre) - RAF

Mum & Dad on their wedding day in Leicestershire, UK, 1963

2
SWIMMING POOLS AND MULBERRY TREES
The Magic and Mayhem of Childhood Freedom

Childhood in Rhodesia wasn't quiet. It was barefoot and loud, sticky with mango juice, penny kools (ice pops) and alive with the sound of cicadas, barking dogs, and children's laughter. Every day was a story, and every season had its own magic. We didn't need much—just water, trees, and each other.

Our swimming pool was the heart of our home. It was where we cooled off in the blazing heat, where we hosted pool parties, and where I learned to trust my body and take risks. That pool saw my triumphs and tantrums. It was my sanctuary, my arena, my stage.

I would dive off the diving board and swim the length underwater, holding my breath, coming up with bursting lungs begging for air. My long blonde hair had streaks of green from all the chlorine, and it didn't matter. My hair would float about my shoulders like a two-tone halo as I contemplated how long I could do an underwater handstand, and if I could beat Andrew's record.

One of my favourite memories is of Dad lifting me onto his shoulders in the swimming pool and launching me into the air. I'd squeal in delight, arms and legs flailing, while Weff clapped and smiled from the edge. I was nicknamed "the fish"—I could swim before I could walk.

From as early as I can remember, we had the most fun on a huge, smooth tractor inner tube floating in the pool. It could hold up to 8 kids at once, balancing in a circle, bobbing on the gentle waves made by us all. We would take turns to try and stand up on the tube without falling off. If you fell off, you were out of the game, and the next one would try to stand up. When we were tired of swimming, we'd get out and lie on our smoothed-out towels or on the baked hot slasto paving to dry off, which was usually about 10 minutes.

We hardly ever got cold in the swimming pool, but occasionally in the late afternoon when the sun was low, we'd be found shivering with blue lips, a fluffy towel around our dripping costumes, but not done with our pool fun. So a "thing" we did was run in the house to the bathroom, run a hot bath with bubbles, and all pile into the tub in our swimming costumes. Usually, as many of us as could fit at once, but it would normally include Victoria, Spencer, any other random friend and myself – and warm up until our skin was crinkled and pink.

It didn't stop there. Once nice and toasty, we'd all jump out and clatter down the hallway back to the pool and dive into the now seemingly freezing water. The shock from hot to cold would give us a second burst of energy and we'd carry on where we left off. We'd sometimes do this a couple of times until Weff would scold us for leaving puddles of water all over the bathroom and hallway. But she was a good sport about it all.

At the end of the day, with bloodshot eyes, exhausted and hungry, Weff would call us out to be wrapped up in big warm fluffy towels and rubbed dry in a cosy hug. Often, I'd crawl onto her lap, wrapped tightly in my towel, her strong arms around me, and I'd fall asleep, spent but content.

The pool was freedom. It was joy.

We lived outside more than in. I climbed trees like a monkey, scraped my knees on tarmac, and picked mulberries until my fingers and lips were stained purple. If I wasn't swimming, I was riding bikes with Andrew, digging in the sunken sandpit, making sandcastles or playing marbles with friends. The world was ours. We ruled it with wild imaginations and a gang of friends within our circle. Getting bellyache was taken in its stride from eating too many mulberries, the trees hanging heavy with large, succulent and shiny-black fruit, bursting with juice.

"Zebbie, have you been at the mulberries again?" Weff would ask, raising an eyebrow.

"Ummm..no? I..." looking down and grinning, with purple-stained lips, purple/blue-stained feet and fingers.

Weff was trying to hide her giggle, with a mock tutting and a shake of her head.

There was no stopping any of the kids who came to visit, either. Running freely around the trees, picking at the abundant fruit.

The orchard held a row of 7 proud, thick trunked mulberry trees, large, healthy, shiny leaves made perfect silkworm food in order to produce bright yellow-orange cocoons for my little pets. The beetroot leaves from Grandma's veggie garden allowed my silkies to spin glorious pink cocoons, which were eagerly traded between school friends.

Below the row of mulberry trees stood a few orange and lemon trees dotted around, which produced, thanks to the climate, whopping-sized, juicy fruit. The grapefruit trees brought forth fruit the size of small soccer balls.

One of my favourites, when in season, was the two naartjie (satsuma) trees standing on either side of the gap in our hedge. So tall, but proudly bursting with the bright orange fruit. It wasn't a good tree to climb to reach the best ones, so I'd politely ask Matthew, our house boy, to lift me up so I could reach them. He was tall, and with a flash of white teeth and a kind smile, he'd reach me down the one I wanted.

The cactus hedge bordering the back of the property would yield a crop of prickly pears. The sweetest, most delicious flesh, but a bugger to pick. Fine barbed hairs surrounded the skin in protection from birds and other pests. You had to avoid getting those hairs in your hands at all costs, but it was almost impossible to escape unless you had help. John, our garden boy, was an expert, though. He would have a tin can nailed to the end of a stick, in which he would reach up and snap the fruit straight into the tin. Then, preparing some newspaper to handle the fruit, he would rub sand all over the outer skin, removing all the hairs. Then, with his sharp pen knife, he would expertly score a slit in the skin and scoop out the inner flesh in one piece, which we would then devour in a matter of seconds. Too many prickly pears, though, were a natural laxative, so we knew when to stop! But they were best harvested and kept in the fridge, to be eaten ice cold on a hot baking day.

Grandma had her special veggie patch, and often we'd go hand in hand to pick gooseberries, strawberries, rhubarb, and little bunches of purple sweet plantain bananas from the banana tree. She'd let me help her dig up the potatoes growing in stacked old tyres, hold my hand walking around the garden, teaching me all the names of the plants and flowers.

In Grandma's side garden was the pomegranate tree. The fruit used to hang low, and we were only allowed to pick the fruit when the telltale sign of ripeness was evident – the outer shell burst open, showing the glistening red jewels inside it.

In another part of Grandma's garden was the granadilla vine, with its glorious purple passion fruit in abundance, decorated by beautiful purple flowers. The guava trees with their yellow waxy fruit with tangy dark pink flesh inside – just picking them from the tree made all the fruit so much sweeter. She had a trellis of raspberries climbing along it, and the pièce de résistance was the large avocado trees. The largest, deep purple thick-skinned avocados, bigger than your hand, would hang low to the ground, bending the branches to almost kiss the earth, the fruit within being a creamy yellow. A favourite snack would be 'sliced avo on toast, a splash of vinegar, a dash of salt & pepper'.

Sundays were for family get-togethers, adventures and making memories. Weff's home-made apple and mulberry pies filled the house with a smell so warm and familiar, it wrapped around us like a hug from the inside out. We'd eat outside under the shade, drink Coke floats, and lie on blankets in the grass while the grown-ups talked politics and we played games until the sun dropped behind the trees.

Grandad Leslie was a mechanical whizz and had an exceptional brain for inventing solutions to problems we encountered. A twinkle in his eye, he doted on his grandchildren, all of us. Grandad's nickname for me was "Chickadee" and it filled me with affection when he called me it.

Chickens chickens chickens! Grandma & Grandad always had chickens, not to eat but for their beautiful creamy eggs. Also, they were ravenous veggie and scrap eaters – nothing went to waste.

It was my job to collect the eggs with Grandad every afternoon. Grandma had a little plastic-lined box which she kept on top of her fridge, in which to collect them. She'd reach down and hand me the box and we'd guess how many we'd find. 6? 7? 8?

Once both Grandma & Grandad came out to watch me carefully collect the eggs, waiting for my reaction to their surprise, they'd planted!

I opened the hen house gate, crawled into the space to inspect the nesting boxes one by one.

First box – no egg. Second box, yes got one! Third box, another. Fourth another. So I went down the line until I'd collected about 7 eggs until I got to the last box. I put the box down so as not to break any, on my haunches and reached into the nesting box and recoiled in shock. There, was the most magnificent shiny empty ostrich egg. I was so shocked, I fell backwards into a pile of chicken poo but didn't notice. I yelled for Grandad, as they both watched my reaction with glee, hiding giggles and mimicking my surprise!

It became my prized possession and once I proudly took it to school to do a "show-and-tell" to my classmates.

After egg collecting, I'd take the eggs to the kitchen, and pick up another box of empty egg shells Grandma had saved, and take them to the manual hand grinder to grind into egg shell powder so we could sprinkle it over the garden beds for the nutrients. Absolutely nothing wasted. Everything had a use.

Whilst we were very little, a perfectly sized Jacaranda tree set the scene for the most wonderful treehouse, which included a tiled roof, proper stable, safe floor and a long ladder operated on a pulley system. The ladder would be floating up high horizontally. The only way to access the treehouse was to use the special hooked stick Grandad created, hook it over the rung of the ladder to pull it down to the ground, ready to climb up. Once up safely, the ladder would gently rise up off the ground again so no unwanted intruders could enter - this included Weff on the warpath! When in trouble, Andrew & I would scoot away and hide in the treehouse, taking the hooked stick up there with us so we couldn't be caught.

Our famous local attraction for miles around, was the motorised contraption designed and constructed by Grandad Leslie, namely the Sandyacht. It was initially built to drive on Beira beach with sails. A large metal frame suspended on fat wheels driven with an engine and steering column with two deckchairs bolted on either side of the engine, a wooden plank stretching from one side of the frame to the other as a makeshift bench to sit on and a canvas just in front of it to put your feet on up out of the way. It could easily carry 10 children for a whiz around our 5-acre garden. It wasn't uncommon to see Andrew chaperoning up to 12 kids at once on the Sandyacht, skillfully manoeuvring around our swimming pool, through the orchard and gap in the hedge towards Grandma's garden, under the Jacaranda trees, past our tennis courts and Grandad's hen house, onto their driveway, which was a large sweeping roundabout. Not only wildly popular with the neighbourhood kids, but often collectively we'd participate in the local annual Jacaranda Festival in town with the Sandyacht as part of the float procession, to raise money for local charities.

The Jacaranda festival was one of an explosion of purple in celebration of the soft velvety petals of the abundant Jacaranda trees of the area. Mum would dress me up in a purple Hawaiian crepe paper skirt and top, purple ribbons tying up my long blonde hair with little purple sandals on my feet. Once the procession slowly started, I'd walk beside the Sandyacht holding tightly to my Grandad's hand, shaking my little collection tin at the spectators lining the streets. Music and cheers of support always, with coins being thrown onto the canvas canopy to catch the donations.

Within our 5-acre property, there was a large piece of ground on the corner bordering the road and Grandad's house, surrounded by massive fir trees dropping pinecones. It was what we named our "spare acre", and where the story of my childhood would not be without it. It was initially used to harvest grapevines and for Dad and Grandad to make home-made bottled wine. I was too little to remember that initiative, so my memory will start with Guy Fawkes. Guy Fawkes was a massive annual tradition for us, which we included our whole community in. Over the course of a year, a property spanning 5 acres produces a lot of excess debris. Grass clippings, trees and branch offcuts, pruned bushes, buckets of pinecones, old tyres, etc, all got piled high in the middle of the spare acre over the course of the year to create a massive mound with the intention of it getting burnt down for Guy Fawkes.

What is Guy Fawkes without fireworks? For this event, Grandad would make an annual trip to South Africa to stock up and import the most amazing fireworks we'd ever seen. Catherine Wheels, rockets, squibs and jumping jacks, sparklers, and roman candles.

Weff, Grandma and any other volunteers would take about 3 days cooking and preparing salads, sandwiches, hot dogs, cakes, tarts, and nibbles for the event, which included all the neighbours, friends, Aunts, Uncles, cousins and included the servants and their families. Grandad would light the bonfire at an agreed time to a roar of cheers. It was totally inclusive - the little children, black & white, waving sparklers around happily making shapes in the dark night. The adults were in awe as suddenly a "screamer" firework would lift off and burst into an explosion of colour and sparkles above our heads amid "ooohs and aaahs". Catherine Wheels would be nailed to a block of wood and attached to a fir tree, out of reach for safety. It would spin on its axis, throwing out coloured sparks as a group of onlookers watched in amusement. Most of the kids and some of the adults had sticks to toast marshmallows and squeezed them between 2 plain biscuits - really delicious.

When the night was over and everyone had gone home, Andrew and I would hunt around the acre with torches to see if we could find the exploded rocket remnants. The next day, we'd be up early, collecting what we could find all over the property, the firework smell still thick in the air. The bonfire would still be burning red hot under the visible black ash and would last for days and days.

Between our two properties, bordering the "spare acre" were a row of enormous pine trees standing strong, tall, and proud, hanging heavy with pine cones. The pine smell wafted over the property with a familiarity I love to this day. Big fat round pinecones would carpet the ground beneath, waiting to be collected in buckets by us kids for Grandad. We would be set a challenge and each handed an empty bucket. For the sum of 50 cents, each bucket would be worth, and Grandad would gladly hand over the pocket money on the production of the bursting pails. Bone-dry pinecones smelled spectacular when used in the roaring fireplace each winter, and would burst and crackle as the pine sap melted in the flames.

Andrew would forever save his earnings, but I couldn't help but spend mine on treats for me and my dolls. Sherbet and liquorice straws were a favourite, as well as Willards Corn Curls (cheese puffs), or the little round perfumed pink sweets called Romantics, we used to use as "medicine" as we played Dr's and Nurses. Flat, round-coloured suckers that came on a strip of 8 that used to shred your tongue to pieces whilst dying it an unnatural colour.

My absolute favourite drink was Sparletta Crème Soda or Cherry Plum – fizzy and sent from heaven, especially ice cold! We used to trundle down to Cheviot Stores, our local little set of shops, for bags of flavoured chips (crisps), a little glass bottle of cool drink which would be drunk and handed back in exchange for the little deposit to buy more sweets.

Andrew, being a very young entrepreneur even back then, used to collect as many glass bottles as he could over a period of time and pile my Silver Cross pram high with the empties, clinking and jingling his way to the shops for his reward. At one time, all the metal bottle tops hid a little styrofoam collectable disk to support a long-running competition run by one of the large distributors. In exchange for several disks, you would win a light-up yo-yo. Not a kid in the neighbourhood didn't have one of these lethal toys, especially as we were learning to master the skills and tricks. Many of us got a crack on the head from a spinning yo-yo.

The local natives held enormous talent themselves. The ladies, locally known as nannies, used to produce the most intricate fine crocheting and needlework, garnished with bright coloured beads. They would walk the neighbourhood with balanced trays on their heads, selling their wares. Table cloths, doilies, wall hangings, aprons, beautiful tops and skirts, and little crocheted beaded dolls of all sizes. They would braid beads into their own hair, wearing bright garments and more often than not, a baby would be strapped to their backs, secured with a blanket or towel.

The men would occasionally ride their bikes with baskets laden with carved wooden trinkets, detailed wild animals and little polished pots with lids, but usually they would leave the peddling to the nannies and children. The men would set up in the towns alongside the road with their chiselled soapstone figurines and elaborate statues carved from ironwood. An authentic sight to behold, seeing Nannies (women) and Baba's (fathers) lining the city streets calling to tourists and locals to come and purchase their wares. Everyone is just trying their best they could to make a living.

Weff & Debra (6) on her 1st day of school

Debra & Spencer in our swimming pool

Andrew (9) and Debra (4) on holiday in Inyanga, Rhodesia

3
ALL CREATURES: BIG AND SMALL

Between Grandmas and our house, just beyond the swimming pool on the side of the "spare acre", grew a massive clump of bamboo. Named "The Bamboo," it was huge, reaching high into the heavens, waving gently in the breeze. It was a favourite nesting ground for the weaver birds, which built intricate woven nests to house their little blue eggs. We would watch from afar as the nests were constructed, their little beaks weaving in and out in the hope of impressing their mate, hoping it was a suitable home to bring forth their chicks.

On trips over to Grandma's, we would see if we could spy any fallen nests, in the hope they would contain broken hatched out shells. Pale blue dotted with little spots was a fabulous find, and I had a "treasure" shoebox full of little trinkets from around the garden, including little shells. Always encouraged to never touch a nest with unhatched eggs in it, but we were also discouraged by Weff and Dad from venturing into the bamboo, as it also housed snakes. The snakes were especially active around the time eggs were in nests, as they were an easy meal. Also, bamboo trunks are covered in very fine, almost invisible needle-sharp hairs and if you so much as brush past them, you can be sure to be squealing loudly, begging for tweezers to pull the little irritants out of your skin. Did we listen? Hell no! The appeal of finding shell treasure was too much, and inevitably it would end in sobbing in the bathroom as Weff tried her best to find and extract the obscured hairs and wipe immense tears simultaneously.

The Bamboo wasn't only home to weaver birds and snakes. It was covered in a carpet of Tribulus Terrestris burs, namely "devil thorns," a small woody seed having long, sharp and strong spines which easily penetrate bare feet or thin shoes like slops (flip flops) and the rubber of bicycle tyres. Most of our childhood was spent barefoot, and often we would forget as we bounded over to Grandma's. As soon as we reached The Bamboo, and accidentally stepped on a devil thorn, it stopped you in your tracks, almost cartoon-like in mid-air, as the pain was immediate and long. Stepping on Lego bricks didn't come close to the pain these barbs inflicted. Leaving deep but small holes in the soles of little bare feet wasn't fun. But we took it as part of African life, got on with it, dusted ourselves off and carried on regardless. We didn't know any different. It was part of our normal.

We'd often find other creatures on the property. Rhinoceros beetles would wander over areas away from human life, but occasionally we'd watch mesmerised as one trundled across our path, its hard shiny protective backs glistening in the sun, its oversized horn leading it ahead. It has wings under its protective armour, and they are strong flyers too. When in battle with each other, they used to hook each other over until the weaker one flipped on its back. They would flip each other out of trees, too.

If you ever come across Matabele ants, you'll know it! Ask any Rhodesian/Zimbabwean and they'll for sure crinkle their nose in disgust. Primarily, termite hunters, but humans are not exempt, as they have a ferocious bite, and 10 or more bites can paralyse a human arm. Its large pincer mandibles would bite the heads off other insects. Matabele ants are named after the Matabele tribe, which originated in Rhodesia, a splinter group of the Zulu. They are one of the world's largest ants, reaching a size of 20 millimetres or more. Another defensive weapon, which is not often utilised, is the sting it possesses. They are known for their raiding parties, which they launch on termite nests. They live in colonies of between 400 and 1,400. When a column of Matabele ants is disturbed, they emit a hissing sound to intimidate the aggressor. Matabele ants will send out a scout in search of termite nests. Once one is located, the scout will return, laying a chemical trail of formic acid. The raiding party then follows this to their quarry. These ants can be seen as a menace to humans, as not much can be done about their abundant existence. You absolutely knew when a Matabele ant had been stepped on because of the foul, pungent, acrid smell which filled your nose, and the air around you stank like a sharp, vinegary burning rubber combination.

Having a sanctuary to let go of all my cares, having the wonderful swimming pool didn't come without its own critters. Of course, hot, dry Rhodesian animals and insects were always looking for water in any form. Dad used to spend a vast amount of his time keeping the pool sparkling clean and bright blue. A long pole with a net on the end would be used to scoop off leaves and grass that had blown in on the wind, especially when the grass was mowed. A pool sweeper would keep the bottom free from grime and grit, and every spare moment Dad had, I'd find him walking around the pool sweeping the bottom with the sweeper. There was a leaf catcher on one side of the pool, which would suck in leaves and grass, too, but there would also be other surprises in store. Lifting the lid of the leaf catcher would always be an event I hated. I cringed every time I was around when Dad did this chore because of what would jump out of there. For a little girl without a care in the world (it seemed), it was frightening to me, so I always kept my distance but was too inquisitive not to watch.

The most frighteningly mesmerising amphibian was the gigantic bullfrog. Thick, warty, rough-skinned and dirty olive in colour, with bright yellow or orange bellies, they revolted me. The males can weigh up to 1.4 kg (3.1 lb) and grow to 24.5 cm (9.6 in) long. They are a voracious carnivore, eating insects and other invertebrates, small rodents, reptiles, small birds, fish, and other amphibians. They are usually found hiding in their underground burrows, which provide them with shelter and protection from extreme temperatures. They don't have teeth, but a hard, bony jaw that can splinter wood.

One of these monstrous amphibians chased Dad once when he fished it out of the leaf catcher, and it petrified the life out of me, thinking that if it caught him, Dad would be eaten. They don't run fast but can jump extensively, between 3ft and 6ft per jump. That is as far as the average man is tall.

My cousin Gregory once caught a bullfrog with our swimming pool inner tube. He threw the ring over the frog like a doughnut, trapping him, and attempted to make him jump out by poking him with a stick. The frog turned on his captor and, with the sound of splintering wood snatched in his jaw, he leapt to his freedom.

Our driveway was a long tarmac strip which led onto a sweeping square on the side of the house, plenty of space for parking or, as us kids often used it for bike riding, go-karting or playing tennis against the side of the house. Weff used to take a daily stroll down the driveway to the post box, which was situated on top of the hydraulic gate, powered by water – another Grandad Leslie invention. This allowed a driver to stay in the car whilst the gate opened, a safety feature for future use! The post box was situated there, so the postman didn't have to come into the yard due to our guard dog, Bully. He was particularly protective and was very territorial, and the postman was afraid of him. So, to fetch the letters, Weff would get the post indoors.

One such trip down to the post box, which was quite high, Weff opened the little door and put her hand inside to feel for the letters. Imagine her shock and terror when, instead of letters, she found a coiled-up Egyptian cobra lying in the warm! She stood frozen, but after what must have seemed like hours, she found her voice and shouted for my dad, who luckily, was home at that moment. He came running down the driveway with his pellet gun and promptly shot it stone dead. A bite from an Egyptian cobra is deadly. When in danger, they rear up and flatten out their head, with their hood protruding on either side of their deadly head. It was huge once uncoiled. From then on, Weff always stretched up and looked inside before sticking her hand inside the letter box.

The forewarning is, if there is one cobra about, its mate is close behind. So, with this knowledge, Dad kept his eyes peeled, waiting for the second one to make an appearance. Sure enough, a couple of days later, he spied it. It had smelt its mate, and Dad shot it out of a tree as it was making its way to the post box.

"Africa is not for sissies", we used to joke. But honestly, jokes aside, you had to be resilient and prepared! Always.

There was a piece of ground on the other side of the house, to one side of the swimming pool, called the "Sunken Garden", where all sorts of flora and fauna used to grow in the soft arid sand. An oversized natural sandpit, mostly the plants and trees which grew there were adapted to a desert-type environment. Cacti and scrub bushes, Frangipani trees with the sweetest fragrance would waft over. I used to pick the little white with yellow middle frangipani flowers and put one behind my ear, and pretend to be living on a desert island. There was a game we used to play, leaping from rock to grass to the steps – "don't land in the river or the crocs will get you!" The best tree to climb was a jacaranda on the side of the sunken garden. I used to jump from the lowest branch down onto the soft sand, getting less brave the higher the branch I'd climb and leap off.

The sand was perfect for making sandcastles, and Andrew once created a whole town with roads and buildings for his dinky cars and tipper trucks, which I was not allowed anywhere near in case I "girlified it with flowers."

But also hiding in this soft sand were little Ant Lions (doodlebugs), insect larvae hidden beneath the surface, waiting to ambush ants and other small insects that fell into their traps. The trap would be a perfectly neat funnel-shaped pit created in the fine sand, which we would often see appear overnight. Being totally curious about the nature we lived in, just like most Rhodie kids at one point or another, we would lie on our bellies, legs bent, swinging in the air behind us as we gently poked blades of grass into the trap. This would trigger the Ant Lion to jump up, thinking it was about to devour a meal. We'd let it disappear, and we would move to the next trap.

One of the most grotesque, bizarre bugs we encountered was the Putzi Fly (Cordylobia Anthropophaga).

If you're squeamish, skip this bit because it makes my skin crawl remembering it!

The Putzi Fly larvae are parasitic. This means that they burrow under the skin of a host animal, where they feed on subcutaneous tissue until they are ready to emerge several days later. Often these hosts were human, causing a condition known as cutaneous myiasis. Its name roughly translates from Greek as "human eater," an accurate nickname considering its meat-eating tendencies. In human habitation areas, people serve as the ideal host for Putzi Fly larvae. The most common method of infection occurs when the female Putzi Fly lays her eggs on clothing that is allowed to dry, such as wet washing on the line, towels, swimming costumes, etc.

The larvae break at the seams before burrowing under the host's skin.

Symptoms typically take up to two days to manifest and can range from vague discomfort and intense itching to insomnia and severe pain. Within six days, the host develops multiple massive boil-like sores. Eventually, these burst, secreting pus, blood, and ultimately the worm itself. You can do nothing to extract the larvae from your skin before the boil becomes "ripe", which is when the worm is usually fully formed. The wriggling of said worm causes the insane itching and the worst thing to do is scratch the boil because you'll send the worm deeper.

There is one way to remove the critter safely, and that is to suffocate it. To do this, you have to smother the top of the boil with Vaseline and cover it with a plaster. The worm then comes up for air and sticks to the Vaseline, and you can then peel the plaster off, and the worm will be attached to it, leaving an impressive hole in your skin.

As a kid, with all the swimming we did, we often used to be subjected to a "Putzi" and some of us are still physically scarred to this very day.

Of course, you absolutely do everything to avoid getting a "Putzi" in the first place. There is only one prevention, and that is to iron every single piece of clothing. The heat of the iron kills the eggs.

All clothes, knickers, bras, underpants, handkerchiefs, towels, swimming costumes, babies' nappies, especially… everything that makes contact with your skin. Because if any of the eggs are left on your clothes, the warmth of your skin will hatch the larvae, and they will burrow straight in.

Weff used to find ironing therapeutic and actually quite enjoyed it. Andrew once got a "Putzi" right on the top of his head from a damp hat that dried after swimming. Of course, it had to "ripen" before he could get rid of it.

I don't think there is anyone I know who grew up in our environment who was not subjected to a "Putzi" at some time or other.

There are numerous other creatures I shared my younger life with.

Shongololos, known as the giant African millipede, were abundant in the rainy season with their thick scaly exoskeleton that would instantly curl up into a tight ball when touched, hiding their thousands of legs in defence. Completely harmless, when danger has passed, they uncurl and go on their merry way.

Flying ants (Ishwa) were, and still are, one of the most popular edible insects after Mopane Worms. Flying ants are a white coloured ant, and when they take to the skies, they do so in swarms by the millions. Harvested usually by the African natives from termite mounds, hunching on their heels over the holes in the ground with nets, or makeshift shopping bags to catch them just as they emerge, the fresh ants are fried, dried, re-fried with salt and water, and then re-dried, creating a double-fried and double-dried dish. The process of drying the ants is important as it removes the wings and legs, leaving only the nutritious bodies. They have a texture similar to popcorn or peanuts.

Mopane Worms are edible caterpillars that feed on the mopane tree leaves, hence the name. They're harvested during the rainy season, then cleaned and sun-dried for preservation. They were a staple protein which made up a meal served with sadza (stiff moldable porridge) & nyama (meat & gravy), and rape (kale).

Wall spiders. My friends, Weff and Dad, would promise me this, and I always used to look for them in my bedroom, feeling comfort when I spied one or two. These gentle, strange-looking spiders were flattened in profile, giving them the common name of Flatties or Common Wall Spiders. They were common in houses, garages, and around large boulders. In the house, they lived on the walls or upside down on the ceiling, in their shades of grey, brown, yellow, and orange, with darker markings on the cephalothorax and spots or mottling on the abdomen. They hunted insects such as mosquitoes, moths, and flies – hence them being dubbed "my friends". They're one of the fastest-moving insects on the planet, and when we used to bang on the wall, they would scuttle for cover behind picture frames or posters.

Of course, they were all there before we were, and my parents were quick to teach us which things we were not to touch or interfere with.

An African rhino beetle

A typical shongololo

Our swimming pool

The Sandyacht

Andrew (13) and Debra (9)

4
FAMILY AND FRIENDS

In my network, nothing was more important than family, but neighbourhood friendships came a close second. They say "friends are the family we choose", and nothing was truer than this in those early days. It's a concept I have continued throughout my life, but in those early days, it was necessary, given the political situation brewing.

You learnt to rely on and depend on each other. Neighbourhoods were close in support, everyone knew everyone else, and when someone needed help, everyone used to rally around collaborating and helping. I remember all the time we would be greeted with a shout, a wave, or a nod whilst out and about.

It was necessary to live like this because often, the women and children were left alone, which meant they were a sitting target.

When kids got ill with chickenpox in the neighbourhood, via the grapevine, Mum would organise "chickenpox parties" so that they all got ill together and it would be wiped out in one go.

Parents would car-share the school runs, go shopping for each other, borrow sugar and milk and return the favour without expectation.

It was customary for us to call non-family adults "Aunty and Uncle" without being blood related. A sign of familiarity and respect.

Often, Aunty so-and-so would turn up unannounced with a cake she had baked and always our kettle would be clicked on whilst she would be welcomed in, ready to exchange the latest information in her circle. It would be reciprocated from Weff, whilst Aunty so-and-so's children played noisily with us.

Other times, we would hear "get your shoes on, we're going to visit Aunty and Uncle so-and-so," and in a flash we'd scramble for our footwear because we used to love to go visiting.

Our circle was made up of many families and friends.

Our blood family included Grandma Win and Grandad Leslie Torry (Dad's parents), Nanna and Grandad Norman Smith (Weff's parents).

The Torrys consisted of Aunty Ann (Dad's sister) & Uncle Val King, kid cousins Liza and Julie.

Aunty Margaret (Dad's youngest sister) & Uncle John Schmidt, kid cousins Pamela, Monica & Nicola.

The Smiths were a much larger family, consisting of Aunty Ann (Weff's older sister) & Uncle John Barnett, kid cousins Dominic, Rebecca, Gregory and Victoria.

Aunty Christine (Weff's younger sister), Uncle Arthur, and kid cousins Damian, Eleanor and Saffron.

Aunty Susan (Weff's youngest sister), Uncle Pete, and kid cousins Spencer and Kirston.

Our "chosen family", ie, good friends, are too many to mention, but they were always around us, visiting, playing, swimming, riding bikes, fishing, and sometimes up to no good too, as kids do. But it was never maliciousness, just mischievous fun contributed by us all. Our next-door neighbours, The Cullens and our Dutch neighbours across the road, The Schaaps. Friends at the top of the road, The Scrutons. More friends further up The Yiend's and The Hatfield's. Other families around The Stantons, The Flowers, The Garrs, The Courtneys.

Victoria was my closest girl cousin growing up, similar in age and in companionship. She and I had similar interests, and as she was slightly older, she would make decisions for us both, and I'd happily go along with them. We'd bike ride in the vlei (open grassland) down to the stream to catch tadpoles in an attempt to watch them grow into little frogs.

We would go on walks together, sharing our sweets and stories. We'd pretend to be grown-ups and make plans for when we were older, dreaming about who we would marry, how many children we'd each have and pick out their names. We would choose our jobs and spend hours painting and colouring cards we'd drawn, or tag along with the boys on our bikes.

Whenever Weff was baking, Victoria and I would be willing taste testers, and we'd share the mixing bowl, scraping the remnants of batter from the sides.

We'd have sleepovers at each other's houses, giggling into the night under home-made forts made from blankets and cushions from the couch and tell each other ghost stories, each trying to outdo the other in an attempt to scare each other.

Weff always made sure she had plenty of tomatoes picked when Victoria was round ours. Her absolute favourite snack was tomato sandwiches with the crusts cut off. Weff would make my banana sandwich without crusts, and we'd be promised an ice cream wafer or an Eskimo Pie (a little block of ice cream coated in a layer of chocolate) for afters.

If we were ever in trouble for something, we'd "run away from home", usually involving disappearing down to the bottom of the garden, set up "camp" complete with campfire, sleeping bags and snacks, determined to not return to the house – until our growling tummies would force us home.

Two of my very close friends were Roelof (Cookie) Schaap and Clyde Scruton. We'd often be found swimming, or baking with Weff, playing with my toys or on the sandyacht. Cookie, as he was fondly known, was Dutch and was the youngest of four, and Clyde was the third out of four boys. Clyde's Mum, Aunty Nel, was a great friend of Weff, often popping in with her boys for tea. Nel was a remarkably tough cookie of a woman, having four rough and tough boys to raise. Afrikaans by heritage, she took no nonsense, a loud, rough diamond with a heart of gold, and necessary colourful language when needed.

She was renowned for going everywhere barefoot. Around her garden, visiting friends, going shopping and even in the city, the soles of her feet were worn coarse and rough. That was just Nellie-Bell, the way she was. Both Aunty Nel and Mrs Schaap used to secretly hope their son's relationship would blossom with me later in life, but our paths were all taken in vastly different directions. Both boys grew up being attracted to men, and I lost my way being so vulnerable and defiant. Andrew used to tease me light-heartedly, accusing yours truly of "turning both boys".

Weff & Grandma with some of our neighbourhood friends, on Grandma's front lawn

Grandad driving the Sandyacht, giving some kids a ride around the garden

5
SHADOWS IN THE SUNLIGHT

But not everything was as peaceful as it seemed. Behind the laughter and games was the ever-present tension of war. We didn't always talk about it, but we felt it.

Grandad Leslie ran G&D Shoes, a little shoe factory with a handful of local employees. Dad worked elsewhere with Uncle Pete, and after work, every day, Dad & Uncle Pete walked to the shoe factory to get a lift home with Grandad.

On one occasion, all the employees finished and filed out of the front office whilst Dad sat observing them. Theft was rife in those days, and everyone was under scrutiny, ensuring nothing had been stolen from inside the factory.

One day, Dad stopped one of the employees in disbelief and asked him to wait behind. After the other staff had left, Dad asked him, "Can I ask, where did you get your shirt from?"

"From my brother, Sir. He gave it to me," came the reply.

It was a crisp, brand-new white cotton button-up shirt, which had a distinctive, recognisable appearance. Dad asked him to let him look at the collar for tag markings, which he complied with. A *"Woolworths, made in UK"* branded label was stitched inside it.

"Well, actually, this is the shirt I got married in, which has recently been stolen from my house. Wait here, I'm calling the police" The identifier was the label and the pattern embellished on the front panels, which Dad had recognised since he had recently bought the shirt especially from Woolworths in Leicestershire, UK, for his wedding day. The shirt had been worn once and then hung up in Dad's cupboard.

The police arrived, did a full investigation, and had indeed found other belongings from our family connected to this employee, which had been stolen in a previous burglary. He was arrested, kept in custody in jail until his court date came around.

When Dad testified in court, the Judge asked, "Mr Torry, is this the person who stole your clothes?" "Yes, it is your Honour, that's the shirt he stole and which I got married in, and he's still wearing it. He informed me that his brother gave it to him, attempting to shift the blame!!"

Being asked by the Judge, "Is that correct, Sir?" by the perpetrator.

"No, sir, I don't have a brother, I lied to him"

"Mr Torry, would you like the shirt back?"

"No, thank you Sir!" to erupts of laughter in the court. He had been wearing it for weeks in jail without taking it off; it was filthy and disgusting, stained with brown sweat and stinking. He rightfully got convicted and served time for being involved in this crime, and was never seen again. Goes without saying he lost his job on the Spot.

Dad was often gone—on a call-up with the army. His absence was a weight I couldn't name at the time, but I felt it in my chest. The nights were darker when he was gone.

One of my earliest memories I have is being bundled into Weff's car in the early hours of the morning, swathed in blankets to keep warm, Andrew in the front, me in the back (Lesley wasn't born yet) for a trip to the Army Barracks to meet the coach of troops, who had been deployed into the African bush for the past several months, in the hope that Dad was actually going to be on the coach and he had made it home. I remember my little heart beating nearly out of my chest to try and spot Dad first before Andrew could, so I could run into his arms in a big swooping hug.

Sadly, some children didn't get their chance, and some wives waited with baited breath, earnestly searching as one by one the troops stepped off the coach. Some wives were left in despair in the car park as the coach drove away, now looking for an explanation instead of their missing spouse. As a 3-year-old, I was oblivious to the wretched panic Weff went through every time we drove to the barracks to meet the coach. Too little to understand the politics behind why he went away for ages, or indeed why. All I wanted was my daddy back, my hero, my protector.

On one of these return visits, Dad returned home without us fetching him, turning up at the kitchen door. A pre-arrangement between them, Weff, with an excited look, called me to say, "Someone's at the door, Zeb (my nickname), do you want to see who it is?"

Thinking it was a cousin or a friend to come and play, I opened the bottom part of the kitchen "stable" door, as I couldn't reach the top. I was left shocked and horrified at the long-haired, stinky, bearded stranger who bent down and whispered "Boo!" to me.

A complete revulsion, I ran away screaming for my mum, panicked and frightened. Their plan had backfired, and instead of the excited little girl he had hoped to scoop up to surprise, it left me screaming and terrified and fleeing for all I was worth. The price to pay for serving your country with a young family: there is a fine line between teasing and trauma.

You need to understand the environment we were living in. Whilst the cat's away, the mice did indeed come and target the homes where the women and children were alone. The locals knew the score. They'd watch and wait. They'd get to know the routines and patterns of when families were most vulnerable. Word soon spread across the towns when the men were called up to do their army service and would be away from home, leaving their women & children alone without their protectors.

So often we had to change up our routine. We couldn't leave the house at the same time every day or take the same route twice in a row. Shopping was done at odd hours—different days, different shops—so we wouldn't be predictable. Friends would drop by unannounced, not just for social calls but as part of a silent strategy: to make the house appear busy, watched, never quite alone. Everyone had guard dogs, and we trained ours to bark at even the smallest disturbance.

Windows were locked even during the day. Doors were bolted behind us the moment we stepped inside. There was a constant tension in the air—a buzzing alertness. You could feel it in your shoulders, in the way your eyes automatically scanned your surroundings, in the way conversations paused whenever an unfamiliar car passed slowly down the street. At the entrance of shops, handbags were rifled through by security guards looking for guns or grenades, prams were searched and often we'd all get patted down before entering to do our shopping.

Children picked up on it, even if we didn't fully understand it. We learned to listen for tone and watch for signs. We became fluent in the language of unspoken worry. And while our games still filled the air with laughter, our lives were shadowed by an ever-present sense of danger—like the hum of an electric fence you learn to ignore but never quite forget.

We had security drills at school. We were taught to duck and cover, to identify suspicious packages left purposely in inconspicuous places, to stay quiet when the alarms went off. Dustbins were regularly scanned and checked for unidentified parcels and all kids' suitcases needed to be identifiable. I didn't fully understand what all of it meant, only that danger was close, and I had to be brave.

I recollect going with Weff to Self Defence classes, sitting on the side of the gym whilst she went through her paces, learning different manoeuvres and stances to get out of emergency situations. As a little girl, watching your soft, loving Mum being put in a chokehold or neck brace by a stranger (instructor) is burned in my brain. Not understanding that it was for her protection, but knowing it was important kept me rooted to the Spot, staying quiet until the lesson was over.

I was a little older when I realised that Weff slept with a gun under her pillow for protection.

The fierce protection she had of us knew no bounds – I was very little when an ice-cream boy (more man than boy) grabbed my hand and wouldn't let me go, and had me screaming for her. In a flash, Weff had jumped the fence, got hold of the ice cream boy and broken three of his fingers. She picked me up, took me inside and immediately phoned the Dairyboard to apologise, but said Don't let me catch him on our street again! "Don't worry, Madam, he's fired as we speak!"

Whilst Dad was away on a call-up, we usually had an armed guard patrolling our property through the night. He'd knock gently on the door every few hours, checking that we were okay. But on one of those nights, for reasons unknown, the guard wasn't there.

We were hosting a sleepover—something we often did with cousins or friends. Andrew and one of our close family friends, Edward, both pre-teens, were excited to sleep in the lounge so they could giggle and chat into the night. Weff tucked me into bed, then turned in herself.

The next morning, I woke up groggy—more than usual. My head ached, I felt sick, and I was freezing. The house was still. I noticed my bedroom light was on, which was strange—I was sure it had been off the night before. As I shuffled down the hallway, stepping over things, I peeked into my brother's room. Empty. Then I remembered—he and Edward had camped out in the lounge.

Their blankets were missing, which I didn't think much of at the time. Maybe they got cold, maybe they built a fort. I opened the lounge door. The boys were still asleep, and the light was on there too. Something didn't feel right, but I couldn't explain it. I went to find Weff.

She was just waking up, holding her head. I crawled into her bed to warm up. When she asked why I was so cold, I told her I had no blankets on and felt sick. She sat up slowly and noticed her light was also on. I mentioned mine was too—and the lounge light.

That's when the realisation hit.

Weff leapt from bed and raced down the hall, calling for us not to touch anything. The boys were groggily waking up. We had been burgled.

She called the police and my grandparents next door. As we waited, we slowly uncovered the chaos: the fridge left open, cupboards ransacked, clothes taken, her prized stash of wool gone—its empty bag tossed in the garden. Weff's handbag had been searched but not stolen. The intruders had taken their time, moving through every room.

When the police arrived, they dusted for fingerprints and pieced together what had happened. "This was planned," they told Weff. "They were in no hurry. Every light was turned on."

Weff, still in disbelief, asked how we hadn't woken up. "You all mentioned pounding headaches and nausea?" One officer said. "They likely had access to ether, a chemical used in anaesthetics. They sprayed it through the house. You're lucky to be alive."

The blankets, we realised, had been used to carry stolen goods.

I'll never forget the way my grandfather turned pale with rage, while my grandmother quietly put the kettle on. Even in shock, she knew what we needed most was a strong cup of tea.

That night marked the end of innocence in many ways. From then on, every door and window was double-checked and locked without fail. Fear settled in like an unwelcome guest. But even in the grip of that fear, life found a way forward. We still played in the yard, still swam in the pool, still played beneath the Jacarandas. We clung to those moments—because in them, we remembered what safety felt like, if only for a while.

Because that's what children do, we adapt. We find light in the dark. And somehow, despite everything, my childhood was still beautiful. It was wild and sweet and terrifying and safe—all at once.

Grandad Leslie set to work rigging up an intercom system between our two houses, using the telephone poles and thick cables on our property. Safety was paramount, and if any further incidents occurred, we could radio through the intercom instantly for help. Just another ingenious way Grandad used his skills and resources to keep his family safe.

I didn't know it then, but I was already learning resilience. I was learning that joy and fear can live side by side. That you can hold on to the people you love even when the world feels shaky. And that sometimes, when everything feels uncertain, you dive into the pool anyway.

Because the water is where you remember who you are. And for me, it was where I felt most alive.

Dad on one of his call-ups, having a rare wash in a tin bath in the bush. His rifle was at the ready right behind him

6
UNPREDICTABLE TIMES AHEAD

Southern Rhodesia, as a sovereign state, was in trouble and soon became Zimbabwe Rhodesia, which was a short-lived sovereign state that existed from 1979 to 1980, after an internal settlement between the white-led government and moderate African nationalists.

Robert Mugabe was elected into Government, superseding Ian Smith and things went from bad to worse.

Vivid memories of being herded onto a school bus with a promise of a "special school trip" with all my school peers, and we were driven to the Capital, Salisbury (which was soon to become Harare).

We were each clutching a little Zimbabwean flag and were ushered off the bus in unison to line the streets, waving our little flags. It was a sea of people, which to me looked so vast I daren't move from where I was put in case I got lost.

Hundreds and hundreds of school children from all different schools around, by the busload full, were ordered to stand shoulder to shoulder, as the new Prime Minister, Robert Mugabe, was slowly driven in his chauffeured limousine. We were to welcome him with open arms, but again, I didn't understand the significance of this moment; I just knew things were going to be very different from now on.

My school soon went from world-class exclusive to second-rate inclusive, and one by one, the change in the curriculum, standards and student ages happened. I was now in a school of diversity with black and white students alike.

Initially, I didn't mind; it was all quite exciting, in fact.

We were all compelled to be accepting, and the majority of us were. Two of my best friends were black and we always played together at break times; colour didn't matter to us kids.

Mercy Mupanduki and Linda Chirawha. Linda was mixed race, so was light-skinned, whilst in comparison, Mercy was very dark, almost blue-black. Linda's Dad was a dignitary in the Zimbabwean government. All we were concerned about was who wanted to play French-skipping or marbles in the playing field.

We used to go about arm in arm, comparing our packed lunches, sharing them amongst the 3 of us and giggling. They were in awe of my long blonde hair, spent ages brushing and plaiting it, I too was equally curious about how dark their skin was and wondered if they too could get sunburnt. We'd stand in line together at the school tuck shop, lining up for our little plastic milk pouches or Bengal juice (chocolate milk) in exchange for the little daily cardboard coupons we were issued.

By the time my sister was born in 1979, my school life was different again.

Non-white students were getting older in classes of youngsters. It wasn't very long before the balance tipped and most of my class were uneducated black older teenagers being forced into the white, exclusive schools, in order to try and force diversity and inclusion, no matter the age or whether they could read or write.

As an 8-year-old, I was soon to be taught alongside 19- and 20-year-old black men, whilst the curriculum had to be re-adjusted to accommodate the majority.

I was being called racial names and harassed by some black students, probably in retaliation for what

they were having to put up with from other older white students. I used to be apprehensive about going to school, especially when the teachers started getting replaced with black staff who inadvertently would side with the same colour students. It was a power struggle which we should never have been subjected to.

Restrictions were imposed and shortages were rife. Initially, I didn't notice it because, as a kid, my parents protected us from all of that. I remember Weff having a little coupon book for petrol. The queues grew and grew, and eventually people were queueing overnight in the hope they could fill up their cars. Word soon spread across the grapevine which petrol stations were getting a delivery, and if you weren't quick enough, you couldn't get close. Good cheese and beef were exported, so we got 3rd grade cheaper varieties. Tools, electrical appliances, whiskey, and toys were in short supply as they weren't made locally. Wheat was hard to come by due to unstable rainfall and seed shortages, and disruptions due to the war and economic conditions, and so was substituted with local flours, which affected the look and taste of bread.

I was 9 when my parents decided to relocate, moving from Waterfalls suburbs (South of Harare) to Marlborough in the North. I moved schools from Frank Johnson Primary School to Marlborough Primary. I used to cycle my bicycle every day on my own to school, but now we were encouraged to cycle in groups for safety, never alone.

The day we moved was the day Weff went into labour and Lesley was born. I was out riding my bicycle with my cousin Victoria that day, having been down to the stream catching tadpoles, and we both were covered in mud from head to toe. I was not allowed near Lesley until I had had a full scrub in the bath and every inch of dirt was off me. It was also that day I discovered a tick on me, picked up in the fields we used to cross to get to the tadpole stream - it had positioned itself in my groin, and when I showed Weff, she had to carefully burn it off with a lighter to stop the head detaching and burrowing in further.

This tick bite marks a significant part of my history and health today, so take note! It will be revisited.

Further substantial changes happened. Street names were replaced, place names rebranded - the country was morphing whilst council services regressed. Salisbury became Harare, Rhodesia became Zimbabwe in 1980 after gaining independence from British colonial rule. The name change was part of a broader transition to a new political and national identity, reflecting the end of white minority rule and the establishment of a new, independent African nation.

Unbeknown to me at the time, Dad had been having issues with his staff at work, and he was becoming tense, edgy, short-tempered, and at times afraid of what life was going to look like in the future.

He was correct to be concerned, as were thousands of other households being subjected to the interrogation and oppressiveness of the tyrant Robert Mugabe. Violence and intimidation were also seen as legitimate levers of social control. Violence was repeatedly used as a political language under Mugabe's leadership in the revolutionary war, against the Zimbabwe rural population and internal dissidents.

We occasionally used to head to South Africa on our family holiday. Money was tight everywhere and with everyone, so most Rhodesian families used to head "down south" on their holidays by car, we were no exception. To fly internationally anywhere was out of reach for most. Having extended family living in Johannesburg and Cape Town, it was convenient for us to stock up on supplies that we couldn't get in Zimbabwe then, due to the restrictions. We'd always get treats too, like boxes of fizz pops and space dust.

Now, due to the political situation brewing in the country, a war in full swing, the only way to travel semi-safely by road was in a long convoy of, sometimes close to 100 cars, patrolling armoured trucks escorting us to the Beit Bridge border of Zimbabwe/South Africa. This was in case we were intercepted by armed terrorists along the way, attempting to ambush any civilians. Safety in numbers.

The plan was to meet early hours of the morning at a checkpoint to start the convoy off, headed by an armed army vehicle with a gunner on the back of it. The rear of the convoy would be patrolled by another armed truck with a third armed vehicle in the middle, all connected by radio.

The middle truck would travel up and down the convoy, keeping a watchful eye in the bush for any sign of movement or threat. At the first sign of anything, the military would be able to deal with it first-hand.

In December 1979, we went on a long-awaited holiday, "down south" to visit family and to stock up on goodies. We took the appropriate precautions, joining the convoy to the Beit Bridge border. I was 9, Lesley was still a tiny baby of just 3 months old.

Well into the journey on the Zimbabwe side, but still some hours to our halfway border destination, Dad suddenly slammed the brakes hard, abruptly screeching to a halt, narrowly missing the car in front. Unexpectedly, the neat convoy of cars was all over the road, jack-knifed as the line was brusquely brought to a standstill. Everyone froze, adults instantly on high alert as the armoured vehicles raced past in communication with each other. Sharp instructions filtered down the line for all civilians to quickly and quietly leave their vehicles and get into the deep ditch alongside the road. Silently. Promptly. The armoured vehicles whizzing up and down, eagle eyes in the bush. Movement had been spotted up ahead, which had sparked action by the troops.

Sitting crouched and hunched in the ditch, you could hear a pin drop. Suddenly, the cicadas and grasshoppers sounded deafening, the dry earth smelled underfoot, the wild scratchy grasses unforgiving on little bare legs.

Hardly daring to breathe, we all heard the army helicopter fly overhead, flying low and circling over one area, and gunshots were fired deep into the brush.

Our own situation was perilous with tiny Lesley, praying she wouldn't start crying. It was hot. Sticky, itchy and slick with sweat, it seemed like hours before the all clear was given for us to get back in the car.

That was enough for Dad to make a solid decision, as did many other families, to break away from the main convoy and put their foot down to get to the border as quickly as possible.

Another trauma which was locked away for a very long time.

Debra (11) school photo at Marlborough Primary School, just before we emigrated to South Africa

7
A NEW FLAG, A NEW FUTURE

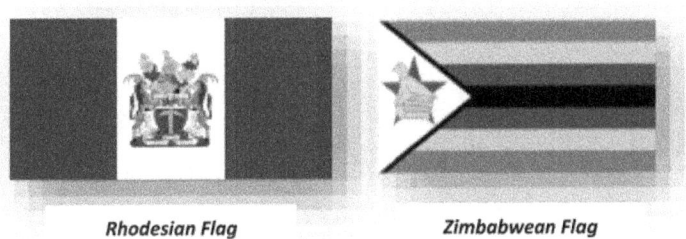

Rhodesian Flag · Zimbabwean Flag

Government laws and restrictions were being made harder and faster, so by the time my parents decided enough was enough, and they made the decision to pack us up and emigrate permanently to South Africa, we were hardly allowed to take anything out of the country. All our possessions were either sold or given away, and our house went up for sale.

In December 1981, we made the big move: Mum, Dad, Lesley and I. I was 11, and Lesley was only just 2.

Andrew, at 16, had decided to complete his high school years by remaining with my Grandparents until he was able to join us in South Africa.

Due to the restrictions imposed on every family leaving the country, our journey South started out with my parents lining the back of our little yellow pick-up truck with all our clothes as a sort of mattress for Lesley and me to lie on.

Dad had an enclosed steel canopy made to go on the back of the truck, which was lockable. We had a little hatch window into the front cabin so we could chat and talk to Mum and Dad as they drove.

Grandad Leslie and Dad modified the truck and engineered a second petrol tank to be welded to the original tank in order that we could continue the whole journey to the border on "one" tank without stopping, especially given our previous experience.

When Dad took the truck to "fill her up", the petrol attendant pumped and pumped and pumped the petrol into the truck, baffled as to where it was all going. Eventually, he crawled under the truck, amazed that there was no leak, and he crawled out, shaking his head, much to the amusement of Dad.

So, we set off South on the 18-hour, 900-mile one-way trip drive in our tiny little yellow pick-up truck.

The little pick-up truck we made the 850-mile trip to South Africa in (minus the canopy)

Lesley and I thought it was a huge adventure, making a bed in the back, nestled in all the clothes and duvets with books and toys. We thought it was great. We had a packed box of sandwiches and drinks, and it was a great picnic, again, not knowing the significance of what was happening.

My job was looking after my little sister in the back, keeping her entertained with stories and playing with her and her toys.

Leaving my home, friends & family, the big swimming pool, the Sandyacht, my Grandparents, and my brother felt like another hurdle, one had no choice but to overcome.

Make it a success - there is no other choice!

Initially, the adventurous journey was oh so exciting. When Lesley had dozed off, I'd lie on my tummy and look out of the back canopy window, watching all the trees go past at lightning speed. I'd wave to the new 'friends' in the car travelling directly behind us in the convoy, also making their journey "down south". I'd try and count the cars in the line, but there were too many and stretched as far back as my eye could see. I remember getting excited when I'd spot the army truck coming past our car on their patrol of the convoy, and I'd wave to the gunner on the back, always with no acknowledgement. I didn't care, as I knew they were there for our protection and they had a job to do. The gunner was training his eye on the bush side amongst the trees and scrubland for any sign of movement.

I'd nod off myself, with the movement of the truck, and the hum of the tyres on the tarmac road. When I got bored of watching the world from where we came from, I'd turn around and face the front.

Weff & Dad were usually in mid-conversation about subjects that didn't interest me, so I'd focus on the scenery we'd yet to drive through. Again, a string of cars up ahead, too many to count. The vast dry bushland on either side of the single tar road we were travelling on, and the many baobab trees with their thick trunks, were dotted here and there. We used to call them the 'upside down trees' as their branches looked like tree roots, and that they should be turned the other way. It brought me back to a memory of the little treasures Dad used to bring back for Andrew and me, from his call-ups when he was stationed in the bush.

He'd surprise us both with items he'd spy with his eagle eyes and keep them hidden until his return. A fruit from the baobab tree - an olive-green velvet seed pod about the size of your hand, inside it was nestled little white nuggets of chalk-like cream of tartar, so bitter to taste, but taste them we did!

One time, he produced from his army rucksack long, beautiful, but very, very sharp porcupine quills. I was fascinated by them, and we still have them to this very day.

He also used to squirrel away an army' rat pack' - the rationed prepacked food parcels the troops were expected to survive on out in the bush with, which included 100 gram packet of rice, a tin of bully beef, a tin of sardines, a packet of 4 ultra hard, almost bulletproof biscuits, a packet of 12 energy sweets, some salt pills to take to replenish the salt lost in your sweat, a silver toothpaste-tube type vessel containing squeezy cheese and another jam, amongst other barely edible things.

He also brought back some kudu and warthog biltong (air-dried, cured meat), and according to Dad, the warthog was the best biltong he's ever eaten, especially when you're starving. One of his troops got permission from the farmer whose farm they were protecting to shoot a wild warthog, and he prepared it and strung it up in a metal corrugated shack to dry out.

But the road trip soon became tedious to this young 11-year-old. I finished my books, I grew tired of colouring in, I got impatient with Lesley when she niggled, and I didn't know how to appease her. Weff and Dad did their very best to entertain us, too, with games of "eye spy" with me and singing nursery rhymes with Lesley.

The longer we travelled as the sun began to scorch overhead, the hotter it became in the back. The little slide windows were open in the canopy; the back window was too. Mum saw to it that we had plenty to drink, but soon I was damp with sweat, sticky and clammy. The African sun, which was so very pleasurable to swim in, was totally unforgiving in this travelling sweat-box.

It wasn't all doom and gloom, though. There were some very funny moments I can reflect back on.

One of these incidents involved Lesley. After getting too ratty in the back and wanting Weff all the time, she was allowed to sit in the front on Weff's lap. There were no safety belts in those days, so it was perfectly normal for her to ride up front. So, finally being comforted by Weff, with her arms around Lesley's little waist, Lesley was happily playing with some toys. Weff turned her attention back to a conversation with Dad. Now, being only a little 2-year-old, little bare brown arms and legs swinging, her hands exploring everywhere, she suddenly put her fingers in Weff's mouth.

Recoiling from surprise, Weff exclaimed to Lesley, "Eeeww, your fingers are wet! Where have they been?"

Lesley replied in her little baby voice, "up my nose!" she said proudly.

Dad was laughing so hard as Weff was urgently grappling for a tissue in her handbag, nearly retching, he almost veered off the road. It was a bright moment which we reflect on to this day, and Lesley often hears this story with glee. Funny times.

Reaching the Beit Bridge border post without incident, it was still several hours having to stand in the hot baking sun before the Border Officer stamped our passports and waved us through to the South African side, to go through the same rigorous process of handing our papers over for a final time to be cleared and branded "emigrated".

The vast crocodile and hippo-infested Limpopo River was nature's division between the two countries, and a solid road bridge connected them.

As we pulled away from the Zimbabwean side for good with a sigh of relief, crossing the river high above the danger below, I'd imagined what it would be like if suddenly the bridge collapsed and we were thrown into the mouths of the crocs. Of course, it was a fleeting thought, only lasting until we got to the other side.

As I watched the gushing river disappear behind us, I was pleased we had made it across safely, and we pulled away unknowing what our future would hold. We were halfway to our end destination, Johannesburg, still hours to go in the hot sun and travelling into the night.

All our worldly possessions were in that little pick-up truck, and we had each other.

Weff woke me up as we arrived at my Aunt and Uncle's house in Germiston. It was dark and unfamiliar. This was going to be home for a little while, in order for us to adjust and settle in. All 4 of us slept in the spare bedroom and lived out of suitcases, sharing household duties with our kind family hosts.

I was unhappy. I struggled to get used to my environment that wasn't mine. It wasn't home. I missed my brother and grandparents, missed my school friends and our pets, missed the freedom I had. In a strange house, a strange country, not understanding the Afrikaans language people spoke (although English was spoken, it felt like it was an inferior language to the minority).

Horrified, Weff and Dad registered me in the local primary school, Germiston Primary, where I knew absolutely no one. The uniform was a dull grey tunic and felt scratchy with a white shirt and tie, very different to the bright green and white cotton checkered uniform I was so used to.

The children in my class were all white, obviously bilingual kids speaking fluent Afrikaans and English.

I was at an immediate disadvantage, standing out firstly because I sounded different when I was brave enough to speak, as I was incredibly shy.

My uniform was brand new, which was a red flag silently shouting "newbie" to everyone else. I also couldn't understand them. A fish out of water is exactly how I felt. Gasping for air. Children can be incredibly cruel to each other, especially if you have an anomaly to pick on – and I was a prime target. Those early months were miserable, and I hated my life but kept it to myself. I knew even at the early age of 11 that my folks had given up their lives too and we were safer where we were. But it didn't stop me from wishing us back to Waterfalls in our old house, as we were before.

My misery lasted about 4 months, when one day, Weff and Dad announced we were moving. They had bought a newly built 3-bedroom bungalow on a plot of land in an undeveloped area called Eastcliff.

It was situated in a lovely little valley, with a hill in front and behind, dotted with huge houses blasted and built into the hillside. Our house was at the bottom of the valley, simple and painted white with a chain link fence surrounding the bare plot. No grass, just bare dirt. Our road was an untarred dirt road prone to flooding like a river when it rained, with a row of houses with some empty plots dotted in between, ready and waiting for new occupants. As bare as it was, it felt different. It felt like a blank canvas that was waiting to be painted a bright representation of a fresh new existence.

We moved into number 12 Olifants Road, Eastcliff, and immediately put down roots in our new life. I was allowed to choose my bedroom, and I made it my sanctuary. Filled it with books and wall posters, stuffed toys and memories of what we had left behind. Lesley had her own bedroom, Weff and Dad in the master suite. It was 1982, and the first time I had seen colour TV.

Very early into our new abode, one day, there was a knock on our front door, and there stood a young girl in a shorts jumpsuit with the longest hair, a smiling face with dimples. Introducing herself in a very English accent as our next-door neighbour, Helen asked if I'd like to come over to her garden to play.

Initially, I was shy but instantly felt at ease with her – she had an infectious giggle and asked if I had ever played swing ball before. I was in awe of her accent and her long hair, and as she handed me a swing ball bat, I instantly knew this was what I had been missing. Friendship. Someone to laugh with, be silly with, swapping books and dreams of meeting popstars, sharing sweets, and playing board games. Our friendship has lasted 45 years, and we have many more times to look forward to.

Weff and Pat, Helen's Mum, soon became friends and Helen and I were inseparable. We saw each other every day. Weff enrolled me in Townsview Primary School, where Helen went, and we continued through High School together.

Both Helen's Mum and Weff worked full-time, so both of us were expected to do our household chores after we got home from school, before our Mum got home. Washing and drying dishes, peeling spuds, hoover the house – just to contribute to helping about the house. Often we'd be doing homework together, then we'd both do Helen's chores, then she'd come over to help me with mine. I still remember to this day that she'd get me to dry all the wooden utensils, like their wooden spoon, wooden breadboard etc, as she had a phobia of drying wet wood. Made her skin crawl. Didn't bother me, so I gladly helped out.

We'd go snooping about the newly built but empty houses on our road, but there was one house that we discovered a rolled-up carpet in it with a dark stain showing through one side. By the time we scooted out of there, we'd convinced each other that there was a dead body rolled up in the carpet and that there must be a murderer on the loose. Our imaginations used to run as wild and free, as much as we used to go about arm in arm exploring our surroundings.

By the time we attended Hill High School together, I'd found more friends around the area that Helen had introduced me to. Leigh-Anne and her sister Bernice (Bobby) were close neighbours on our other side, Loretta and her family neighboured us behind, and Celeste up on the hill behind them. Avril, Marina, Ana, Rodney, Richard, Danny.

Making my way through High School was not without hiccups, but was relatively pleasant, learning the basic language skills in Afrikaans in order to award me a pass. My grades were middle of the road, not failing anything, but not excelling in anything either. I worked hard, especially enjoying art as a subject and swimming as a sport. Sport was compulsory in our curriculum, often finishing late in the afternoons. I made the Swimming Team, Tennis Team, played table tennis, netball and sometimes hockey. The school days were long but productive, and mostly made well-rounded, grounded young adults. We were expected to conduct ourselves with decorum, respect and adhere to all the strict school rules. If you broke the rules, they broke your spirit. The teachers were strict but kind. But step out of line, and they'd dish out physical punishment and detention without concern.

Boys would get caned on their backsides, as did the girls across the hands. One teacher, whose reputation is burned in my brain from fear, happened to be an Afrikaans teacher. She used to wield a long, thin shambok-type stick (thick at one end, tapering to a thin point) wrapped with red insulation tape. God help you if you were subjected to any punishment from this weapon, for something as little as talking in line. If only one person was caught talking in line, everyone in that line got caned – you were expected to have each other's back and work as a team. So, if one person let down the class, the class got punished. And if that happened to be you, God help you after that class and at breaktime, as you'd get lynched by your classmates. Teamwork, discipline and respect were order of the day.

But we had some funny teachers, too. Miss Teper was allergic to citrus, so the boys in our class were compelled to bring oranges to class and spray the oils into the air. It subjected her to such fits of sneezing that she couldn't teach, and we often used to get a free Accounting lesson those days.

Mr Natas who taught Mathematics, had a different coloured tie for every day of the year, the Geography teacher Mr Scott who was a huge bear of a man with just the kindest heart and gentlest voice but led the boys Army Cadets and transformed into a booming loudspeaker all of his own, barking commands to the scholarly troops, and Miss Jay our swimming coach who worked us hard and fast training the team to compete in interhouse and interschool galas.

I loved our teachers in very different ways, and I am still in touch with some of them to this day. It was with mixed emotions that we all Matriculated and spent our last day of school signing each other's uniforms and yearbooks, swapping phone numbers to keep in touch. 1982 – 1988 were fun-filled and surrounded by many school friends and acquaintances.

In hindsight, looking back, I lived a protected, somewhat sheltered life, being protected by my parents. An extremely close family dynamic, not surprising that Weff and Dad wanted to shelter me from the world's horrors, gauging given what they had seen. There were strict rules at home, too. I wasn't worldly wise, never went clubbing or drinking, never ever smoked or hung out with "the in-crowd", and I was still painfully shy.

I had just turned 18 and my life was about to take another tense and dramatic turn.

Thirty years later, I travelled to our 1988 High School Reunion in Johannesburg, and it was as if no time had passed between us, yet we had all been projected on different roads of discovery. Time had not been kinder to most, as living in a deteriorating country subjects you to stress and hardship that you don't realise you're under when you're living in it, but the worry lines tell a different tale. Stress levels and living with a permanent adrenaline-fueled body eventually wear you down to the ground, and I was just about to discover this myself!

A baobab tree which bears the fruit containing Cream of Tartar

Helen (L) and Debra (R) aged 11 – My best friend and next-door neighbour, still very good friends 45 years later.

Visiting Helen in Newcastle, UK in 2019

Duncan Cheerleaders at our Inter-house sports day Sports Day at The Hill High School. Debra (3rd in the back row)

Debra (18) at the Matric Farewell (Prom) in 1988

8
A WOLF IN SHEEP'S CLOTHING

Have you ever had the deep desire wishing you could turn back time? Have you ever woken up one morning and thought, "This is not the life I expected!" You regret the way your life has played out in front of you, and you feel you've not had control of your decisions. The many people who have been scarred along the way based on your defiance and ultimately your choices?

Well, dear Reader, if you have got this far, brace yourself for what was about to be one of those times in my life in which I'd love to turn back that clock.

After I graduated from high school with decent grades, my intention was to go to University and I enrolled on the Fine Arts Degree course. As things went, my enrolment got erroneously mixed up by the Uni (by their own admission), and they oversubscribed the course, and I wasn't enrolled. I didn't know it at the time, but it's a shame it played out this way, as it seems I have a natural talent for art. It comes naturally to me, and I've surprised myself without having to try too hard at successful projects.

So, I did the next best thing: I enrolled at the local Academy of Learning and completed an Executive Secretarial Diploma, gaining a 98% average. The experience I gained in typing, shorthand, organisation, and communication skills set me up for future employment. The college class was small, only about 9 of us, and we quickly became good friends, socialising in and out of lessons.

One such character was Wendy, a bright, bubbly red-headed teenager with a shock of tight curly hair. Similar in age to me, nothing seemed to faze her, and she always had her infectious giggle at the ready. I was envious of her two deep cheek dimples, which made her face beam like sunshine and she brightened up any room. It was good to be in her company and we bounced off each other with hilarity.

On a fateful day, Wendy asked me if I would go on a blind date with her and her boyfriend, Deon, as they had someone they wanted to introduce me to. Deon, in his early 20s, was in the army and was based at the barracks quite near to us. The blind date was an army friend of his who was looking to meet new friends in the area. I thought nothing of it and agreed to go as a friend.

Never having had a relationship before, being totally naive, I was looking forward to having an evening of chatting and getting to know him. Sadly, on the day of the blind date, Wendy broke the news to me that the friend had had an accident and couldn't make it. I was disappointed as I was looking forward to it; however, she quickly reassured me that Deon had asked someone else at the barracks who had agreed to step in at the last minute.

I often wonder where I'd be now if the initial friend had made the date because life was about to get the better of me in the worst way.

Wendy and Deon picked me up from my house, and Peter was in the back of the car. He was dressed in his army uniform, as was Deon, because they had come straight from the base. I slid in the back next to him, really shy, but he held out his hand to introduce himself. Totally pleasant with a cheeky smile, the four of us made small talk with lots of laughs and giggles. Peter was Afrikaans, English being his second language, but he spoke it quite fluently. We had a very pleasant evening, and when they dropped me off at home, he kissed me on the cheek and said how nice it was to meet me. He had impeccable manners, and I glowed inside; I thought he was such a nice guy. I quickly made up my mind that if they asked me, I'd go out with them again.

At college the following day, Wendy pumped me for information about my thoughts on Peter. I eagerly told her how I really enjoyed his company and how I had enjoyed myself. So, she quickly set up another date for us, and this time he was eager to learn more about me. I told him all about my family, background, school days and our life in Rhodesia. He hugged me, and it felt pleasant, so when he casually slung his arm over my shoulder, it felt natural. He was exuding charm and charisma, and it soon turned into future dates. Most of the time, he came dressed in his army uniform as he would pick me up straight from the army base. He was full of praise and compliments, making me feel so very special. "I only have "ogies vir jou. Jy's my little lady" I only have eyes for you. You're my little lady."

I graduated from college and lost touch with Wendy as she took up a job somewhere.

Peter continued to visit, and his demeanour intensified, becoming protective, attentive, and focused. He'd make plans for us, deciding for us both. He'd sulk if arrangements didn't go as planned. Not having been in a relationship before, I sorely misjudged it for caring and affection, and soon I was smitten with this young man. Everything he talked about was about us and our future. He promised me that he'd look after me and wouldn't let anything hurt me ever. He told me he wanted a family one day, but there was plenty of time for that. He painted an idyllic outlook which was totally achievable with hard work and dedication. I was in.

He met Weff and Dad, and was respectful but reserved, somewhat distant. Weff tolerated him only for my sake; Dad detested him. I couldn't understand it. To me, he was so lovely, caring, kept me safe, and made me feel special. Dad said he gave off vibes that he couldn't explain, that there was just something he couldn't put his finger on; it was a gut feeling. I put it down to growing up in a different household, ours being English, and it was his Afrikaans upbringing.

I met his parents. He had a large Afrikaans family, six brothers and sisters. His older sister was married, and they had two children, but they lived across town. Initially, she took an instant dislike to me, which was disappointing, but it was her right. I'm not everyone's cup of tea, but I usually get on with most. Another younger sister of Peter's was also married, and they had one child, but they all lived at home with his parents, as did the rest of the brothers and sisters. Peter's mother was a quiet woman, speaking mostly when she was asked a question. She had an air about her that she had lived a very hard life and that she had had to fend hard for herself and her kids. She was bent over as if she had had the world on her shoulders for years, and her face was deeply etched. She was dishevelled most of the time, a characteristic "huisvrou" *housewife*.

His father was a large, imposing, daunting bully of a man, with black, greasy hair slicked back, with a permanent scowl and an overbearing aura. All Peter's siblings, including himself, feared their father, and so they should have. He was aggressive and bullish. He was an inebriated alcoholic, and the day I met him, I could smell him from across the room. Peter ushered me into to their gloomy, untidy living room the day of initial introductions, and his father was sitting by himself watching TV, beer cans and a whiskey bottle next to his recliner.

"Pappie, this is Debbie. I just want to introduce you to the girl I'm going to marry one day."

His father sat up slowly, leaned forward to scrutinise me top to toe and said in a slurred bellowing voice, "Dit sal die donnerse dag wees!!" *That'll be the fucking day!*

Peter quickly ushered me into the kitchen to sit down with his Mum and siblings. No one wanted to be in his company. One of the sisters made me a cup of coffee, and the rest of them started asking questions about where I lived, where we met, do I work, what I'd like to do in the future, all the usual queries people ask when they meet an older brother's girlfriend. I soon relaxed a little as his Mum told them to stop barraging me with questions, and with a tired smile asked me if I'd like to stay for dinner. We'd been driven in Peter's car, so I was reliant on him to drive me back home, so I felt obliged to and thanked her, asking if I could do anything to help.

"Nee nee" *no no*, "tell me about your "familie" *family* and we chatted around the table through dinner. Not another sign of his father, he was sitting alone in the lounge with only alcohol empties for company.

Time plodded on, and I got sucked further and deeper into Peter's world. He'd got into a routine, picking me up from home, and I'd spend weekends with him and his family. It was a loud, bustling household of 8 family members, 10 including us when we stayed. It was cramped and busy. I did all I could to help his Mum with the chores, as did the other siblings, and we got into a routine of who was allocated certain tasks. I usually washed the dishes or helped hang out the washing on the line. Heaps and heaps of washing for the whole household.

Developing a relationship with this dysfunctional family, whilst Peter was promising me the world, being super attentive and basically hoovering my emotions, my relationship at home started to break down. I was becoming more defiant; I would backchat Dad about me going out with Peter, and of course, Peter would fan the flames in manipulation and ask me, "Who's in charge of you? You're an adult now, you can do as you like, and nothing is stopping you. Stand up for yourself because if you don't, you're going to lose me, and you'll cause me to walk away. I'll move on!" That absolutely panicked me, and it was like a snare around my immature adolescent heart.

Peter didn't ask me to marry him, he told me we're going to get married one day, and I believed him.

Why wouldn't I? He'd meticulously assured me bit by bit that if I cooperated, it was totally achievable. By this time, my feelings weren't my own, he'd already got me on a string like a puppet, bombarding me with affection and compliments. I felt special, wanted, needed in a dependent kind of way. I got played like a fiddle without even knowing it. Sometimes it felt smothering, but I shook off the feeling, putting it down to hormones, loneliness, tiredness...anything I could think of. What I didn't do was share my feelings with my parents, like I should have done.

However, one significant conversation I remember having with Dad was about marriage. Peter and I sat down with Dad (my heart pounding and gushing in my ears), and he announced that he wanted to get married. I sat in silence, embarrassed and already anxious around him to speak up. I hung my head in nervousness, clenching my jaw and wiping my sweaty palms on my trousers.

I can't imagine what went through Dad's head, but it fell on deaf ears. He didn't give us his blessing, he pleaded and implored us to wait a couple of years, suggested an engagement instead, but no, Peter was having none of it, totally adamant and out of earshot of Dad, he made his feelings known. He was determined to have his way, and I was at risk of losing him if I didn't go along with it.

Weff tried her level best to explain things to me, Dad did everything to try and dissuade me from being with him, and the more intense it got at home, the more Peter drip fed me his opinions about how, "They're ruining my relationship with you, they're too controlling, I can't and won't be without you, how about now you've finished college you move out and move in with us? I'll be out of the army in a couple of months, so it won't be for long. I can get a job and then we'll find our own place." He painted a life of success, fulfilment, and independence.

Peter's logic was that since I spent nearly every weekend with his family, unbeknown to me, he'd already taken the liberty to ask his mother on my behalf who had agreed to let me stay. His father hardly bothered who was in the house as long as he had his "dop" *alcohol*. He just didn't care. Alcoholics never do.

Neither do Narcissists, apparently.

FACT

"Narcissists may show you love and act in loving ways, but this tends to be conditional, in that displays of love depend on what you can give them in return. For people with NPD, relationships tend to be transactional."

https://psychcentral.com/health/types-of-narcissism

9
TOXIC ISOLATION AND WALKING ON EGGSHELLS

The estrangement of a daughter from her parents can, in some instances, be read as a mark of immaturity on the part of the youngster, who may not yet have experienced the emotional challenges of parenting.

I'll never forget the day I broke Mum and Dad's hearts. That memory sticks in my throat as if to suffocate or strangle me, and it's from this point that my world truly unravels.

It was a Friday. Weff was on a trip back in Zimbabwe to visit Nanna and her sisters. So, it was Dad, Lesley and I at home. After a particular confrontational conversation I'd had with him, Peter laid a final ultimatum at my feet. "You move out or I'm gone."

I begged him to reconsider; my heart was aching, feeling like I was being torn down the middle in two. He stood firm; he wasn't prepared to compromise or negotiate.

The conversation ended, and I turned on Dad ferociously. I felt trapped, and Peter had convinced me it was Dad's fault that I couldn't make up my own mind. He accused me of being weak and "being under my father's thumb". He ended on "good luck in finding anyone else willing to give us what I had planned for us – remember you threw us away!" he viciously provoked.

Against my better judgement, I shamefacedly told Dad I'm moving out. That was it, I'd made up my mind in a panic. I had been promised the world, I wanted my independence, and Peter was dangling it like a carrot before me blindly. I became rebellious and stubborn. Peter had hardly given me any time to think thoroughly – a tactic I now know was deliberate.

Both of us, shouting at each other, said some hurtful things which we didn't mean (and I take every single one of them back), and I know Dad regretfully declared, "If you leave, you don't come back!" Dad was trying everything to get me to stay and see reason.

I wasn't about to change my mind, hot, defiant tears burning down my cheeks and splashing on my shirt. I threw some clothes into bags, crammed as many things in as I could so I wouldn't have to return, and I was ready for Peter to pick me up. As soon as I got in his car, I literally felt my world collapse and off he sped to his mother's. I cried the whole journey there and felt dread settle in my chest.

Settling into a manic household, I didn't have time to dwell on what had just happened. I slipped into a busy routine, helping to cook, clean, wash, hoover, mop, and go grocery shopping with Peter's Mum and sisters. I was happy to help, as of course they had let me stay for nothing, and I was another mouth to feed. There was always something to do. It was very evident that the women in the household were expected to wait hand and foot on the men. It was embedded in their culture. Orders were barked, certain chores just simply expected and like mini robots, we just got on with them.

Peters' ongoing behaviour changes started subtly, but he very quickly became controlling, possessive, and insanely jealous. His demand for attention was incessant, constantly seeking my reassurance and praise. He'd get offended and easily hurt at the slightest inkling if he thought my attention was directed anywhere other than on him, and he'd focus excessively on his own wants and needs.

Occasionally, he'd throw me a bone of adulation or approval for something, and I'd hang on to those moments, attempting to please him every moment I could in order to feel worthy enough to be with him.

Those moments of praise would always be in a room full of people, making me feel embarrassed and shy. Never in private, behind closed doors. This I now know was to show everyone what an adoring person and later husband he was, therefore turning the focus back onto himself. A real Jekyll and Hyde.

Seeking the security and safety that I had foolishly surrendered with my parents, Peter made the arrangements for us to get married quickly in the local registry office. There was an issue with my age, as at 19, I was still underage, and I needed my parents' consent in order to legally obtain a marriage license. Peter dealt with that by forging Dad's signature so that he didn't have to revisit that conversation. No way was he prepared to confront that issue again. He'd convinced himself that he'd already won that battle.

The date was set, plans were made, and I numbly just let it happen. Weff and Lesley came to support me and try to talk me out of it one final time. Dad refused to attend.

By this time, I was in a deep depression, hollow and unthinking, and it was easier to let it all go ahead than face the fight with his family to call the whole event off. In such a short space of time, I was a shadow of my former self, not caring about anything. I'd lost weight, was pale and unkempt.

♥

You ask, "Why didn't you leave then?" but I had nowhere to go, no income and no home to return to. Also, when you are being manipulated, you cannot "see the wood for the trees", and a dark cloud settled around my world. I looked to him for the promise of love and support, and I got delivered coercion, humiliation, and segregation.

♥

A trauma bond had developed with me, as Peter provided sporadic gifts throughout our relationship in the form of affection and devotion. In the initial moments of our relationship, he showered me with attention and love, a process referred to as "love bombing."

This love bombing process sends the feel-good chemical dopamine levels skyrocketing within the brain, and that's when the partner develops a strong attachment to the narcissist. I felt as if I was the love of his life, and that I had found my perfect partner.

Once he showed his true traits, however, I was desperate to get the love and attention I had initially been given in the beginning. It got harder to please him, and yet again, I'd feel a dopamine surge when he showed me bits and pieces of affection. This pattern is a recognised tactic used by Narcissists.

I feared Peter at this point, and I did my level best not to anger him in any way, convinced I'd be blamed for being ungrateful for everything they'd done for me. After all, I'd been conditioned to think that Peter was my last hope of having a partner, as "no one would want second-hand used goods." My days consisted of being belittled, downtrodden and made to feel worthless. Hence, I tried to keep a low profile and slink into the background, treading carefully with my words and actions.

The abuse started early on, but cunningly so that I (and others) wouldn't notice it. It started verbally with name-calling, teasing, and excluding me from conversations spoken in Afrikaans, in order for me not to understand them. His brothers and sisters would whisper about me to each other whilst I was in the room. I knew enough by this stage to know the sinking feeling when they switched from English to Afrikaans, with side glances in my direction.

Abuse comes in many different forms, whether it's coercive control, psychological/emotional, physical, financial, verbal, and sexual, and I was subjected to the motherload once that ring was on my finger.

I was now his to do what he liked with, often being told "I belonged to him now, I'm his property as he is responsible for me", his possession to keep under control, to keep isolated from my support network and to keep him fed and watered.

If he so much as assumed I'd stepped out of line, I'd get an absolute verbal grilling followed by a backhand to the mouth or a fist to the stomach. But it was always followed by apologies and tears and promises of it never happening again, if only I didn't make him so angry, he wouldn't lash out.

Another element of this toxic environment was that the whole household were compulsive gamblers.

Horse racing was the order of the weekends, morning till night. They would place bets on every horse race without fail, the radio blaring out the commentary and results. The arguments that were had, convincing each other that he/she had the best odds, were at crescendo levels sometimes. Convinced their earnings funding the habit of course would be replicated in winnings, which hardly ever came to fruition. In fact, the opposite happened; the constant losing led to extreme frustration, which bled into aggression and everlasting debt.

Peter was still in the army completing his 2-year mandatory training, and was paid a pittance, which he would begrudgingly give his mother towards household bills. There was never enough money, and our belts were tightened every month.

I offered to look for a job, but very quickly, I was informed I would not be working. Peter would be supporting us both when he completed his basic army contract, and he'd find a job to save up and move out. Conversation closed! Not to be discussed. EVER.

Army contract completed, Peter found employment as a gear-cutter in an industrial factory, with a decent wage, more than enough to cover our bills, if gambling didn't drain his pay packet every month. There was no spare money to save for us to move anywhere, as his

Mum would borrow from him, his father would demand money off him, and he'd gamble the rest away. I felt like I was always walking on eggshells, too scared to question, too nervous to ask, so I just let it be.

Behaviours became intensely frayed within the household between him and me. Peter would set rules for me to abide by when he was at work, and if I didn't, he'd sulk for days, followed by intense rage.

I was not allowed to go anywhere on my own; I always had to have a chaperone in the form of his mother or siblings, and they were instructed to report back to him where I'd been and who I had talked to. I badly misread the signs, thinking it was "being looked after and kept safe" instead of "controlled and manipulated".

Thinking back, I was not street-wise, never had to be, always being protected by my parents growing up, so innocence was only natural. Never did I dream there were such monsters in this world.

No telephone calls were allowed whilst he was at work, as he couldn't monitor them.

No makeup or tight clothes were permissible because "you're not a whore to walk the streets when I'm not with you."

I was not allowed to mingle with the male members of the family; the women remained separated at functions like braai's (BBQs) or parties, and I was expected to follow suit.

I was totally banned from contacting any of my family, and all my friends faded away - I lost contact with everyone.

When I refused to indulge in the weekly betting frenzy, I'd be ridiculed and mocked. I had no money of my own and no income as I wasn't allowed to work, so I pretty much became a recluse, hollow and empty with very little emotion. I was just there, in the background, nondescript. I was well on the way to being conditioned to accept what was delivered to me, whether it was a compliment, an order, or a back-handed slap to the face. But the isolation kept me trapped. I was turning into his mother.

It was many years later that I first understood the word Narcissistic Personality Disorder (NPD) – I had no idea what living with such an ogre was like.

> **FACT**
>
> "If the victim can't go to work, don't see family, can't leave the home, or access a phone, they are kept vulnerable to the abuser and the abuser's version of reality.
>
> People living with NPD can be abusive in ways that interfere with their relationships. These behaviours can range from hurtful and unwarranted criticism from a perfectionist employer to life-threatening physical attacks from an enraged intimate partner."
>
> https://www.medicalnewstoday.com/articles/narcissistic-victim-syndrome

Then his father lost his job that he was barely hanging onto between bouts of binge drinking, and I was directed by him that I needed to contribute towards the household finances. I was happy to as it might have given me an outlet somehow.

However, a monumental argument ensued between father and son, but Peter finally backed down under threats from his father. Learned behaviour came full circle, but it was too late now. I'd made my bed; I had to lie in it.

I applied for some vacancies and successfully landed a data analyst role at South African Eagle Ltd, an insurance broker. It was a junior role, but starting with a fair wage. I could now put my qualifications to use and start saving to move out of the household of 10, and get some much-needed daily distance between me and this unconventional family.

We found a 1-bedroom ground-floor flat, as luck would have it, in the centre of the town right opposite the company I worked for, which was a Godsend! Affordable, it was very convenient and didn't eat into my salary with travel expenses, as I could just walk across the road and I'd be there. Monday to Friday, no weekends. It was just perfect.

Thinking that this would be the change we needed, that things would calm down and start on the upward turn, how very wrong I was. The abuse only intensified.

The verbal humiliation and financial control doubled overnight, but still I thought "if only I could behave how he wants me to, he'll change" It must be my fault that got him angry all the time, maybe it was the way I answered his question? Maybe it was my tone? Maybe I said the wrong thing? Maybe it was the way I looked him in the eye? I'll try harder next time.

By far the worst of the abuse was the intimate control and sexual abuse I was subjected to by this unfeeling monster. The intimacy was always on his terms and he had an extremely high sexual drive. There was literally no choice but for me to be obedient, "lie back and take it" until he was finished, as my protests were useless. He hurt me in more ways than I can describe. Physically and emotionally, and in those times my mind would escape to the swimming pool, sandyacht, or treehouse when I was little. Silent tears would leak out of my eyes as I rolled over into the foetal position, knees up to my chest, as he rolled the other way and fell right to sleep. If he caught me crying, I'd get berated for "crying like a baby, for God's sake, grow up, you're a big girl now!"

I'd lie awake quietly sobbing until I heard him snoring, which is when I would gently slip out of bed and go to the bathroom to clean myself up and stop myself from losing my stomach contents into the bowl.

He'd "surprise" me by throwing some cushions and our duvet on the living room floor, snacks and crisps ready, setting it out like having an intimate movie night together – and then he produced the porn videos he'd somehow acquired. In a sick turnaround, he'd attempt to re-enact certain scenes whilst the movie was playing. "Just practising," he'd snarl, sometimes with implements that would make me bleed. I couldn't even rely on my monthly putting him off; in fact, it spurred him on.

After the first time, I shuddered when he'd announce his "surprise" for me, and I never knew when that was.

I wondered what I'd done to deserve such treatment, but I was powerless to do anything about it. No support, I was too embarrassed and beaten down to talk to anyone about what was happening. Naively assuming that maybe this is how things were supposed to be, and some nights I'd wish I'd never wake up, but of course, the nightmare didn't end.

During one vicious session, he had verbally reprimanded me over something trivial and motioned to the bedroom. I had just come home from work and was tired, but it didn't faze him. He nodded at the door, which was my cue to get my ass in there, but I stood frozen to the spot. I couldn't move; my body just wouldn't cooperate. So, he grabbed my arm and frog-marched me into the bedroom and threw me onto the bed. He had a look on his face that said "don't argue, just don't even go there", but from somewhere I found the strength to voice my plea to have a break. I was sore from his past sexual episodes, which were so rough and frequent, I was red raw and in pain. A strange calmness crossed his face; his eyes clouded over with a blackness I'd not noticed before, and he broke out into a slow, sick grin as he wrapped his fingers tightly around my throat, pushing me hard into the mattress and kneeling on my thighs. I openly sobbed, begging him to get off me, but I got a severe whooping for that after he finished, and that night, I died inside.

Never would anything be as bright or lovely. I never challenged him again.

> **FACT**
>
> "The phenomenon of 'narcissist black eyes' has captured the attention of many who have encountered individuals with Narcissistic Personality Disorder (NPD). This intriguing concept refers to a perceived change in a narcissist's eyes during moments of intense rage or manipulation."
>
> https://www.ourmental.health/narcissists/the-phenomenon-of-dark-eyes-in-narcissistic-individuals

I had been in my job 3 months when I came down with the flu, diarrhoea, and generally felt unwell. I persevered at work because being there was far preferable to being at home. But eventually, I was forced to go to the doctor who delivered the news, "Congratulations, you're pregnant." I was 19.

As soon as I was told the news, once again my world spun, and I vowed that I was going to do anything to protect this little life from any hurt from anyone. It felt like I had been thrown a lifeline and that I would do what it took to shield this little one from the hurt I'd been subjected to. A mother's protective instinct kicked in instantly.

As my belly swelled, Peter changed tactics and became very hands-off but ramped up the verbal berating, gaslighting me at every opportunity. I thought I was honestly going mad. I'd question my behaviour all the time, wondering what I had done, what I had said, did I say what I meant, how could things have gotten so turned around? He verbally and emotionally tied me in knots, accusatory and wild with jealousy, almost manic with possessiveness. During my pregnancy, he would boast to everyone that he was going to be the most wonderful Dad. He was convinced I was having a girl and for nine solid months never failed to tell me he hoped he'd made a girl.

My feelings didn't count; he made it all about him. I was not allowed to choose the baby's name; that privilege was given to his mother. A girl's name was picked out; a boy's name was not considered or discussed.

Still, the ground rules applied to me, even more so, as he now used to time me to get home.

As we lived just across the road, it wasn't far to walk, but he started timing the walk home. At clock-out, he'd give me one whole minute to get from the office desk to the home front door. As I grew bigger and more swollen, I'd waddle as fast as I could to get home before his curfew. If there was a hold up somewhere, like a last-minute customer call or one of the Managers needed something doing, I'd be petrified about what was waiting for me when I got home. He immediately wanted to know "who did you stop to flirt with today?" and "how long has the affair been going on?" Such paranoia was insufferable.

I am extremely time sensitive to this day because of this PTSD, and I cannot be late for any appointment; otherwise, unbearable anxiety and panic set in.

If we were going anywhere in the car, if I dared to look out the passenger window and he saw someone walking on the pavement, he'd be convinced that I was ogling them and that I was such a whore.

On one workday morning, my manager called me into his office to discuss the excessive incoming phone calls blocking up the phone line, by Peter. I broke down and explained my home situation to him. He was mortified and very understanding, but implored me to have the conversation with Peter that he was able to call me, but during my lunch hour.

Dread and panic set in as I waddled home that evening. It did not go well. I was accused of having an office affair and that I was somehow trying to stop him from knowing where I was at all times. His parting words to me that next morning, as I left for work, were "Don't come home tonight unless you've resigned."

I had no choice but to follow his instructions. I sat down with the same manager and poured my heart out to him, and unfortunately, I have had to give in my notice. It was accepted reluctantly.

I was now out of work, heavily pregnant and had debts to pay for. He regularly gambled his earnings away, so we were living hand to mouth on my salary. We couldn't afford to keep paying rent, so back to his mother and father we moved.

> **FACT**
>
> "Many times, we are blind to the manipulation tactics and narcissist control tactics that the people we love use against us.
>
> These Manipulation Tactics and narcissist control tactics work to erode, suppress, subjugate, and degrade the victim's sense of self and diminish their social standing in an effort to dominate and control."
>
> https://abusewarrior.com/mental-health/manipulation-tactics/

10
WELCOMING BABY TAMARA

My world changed for the better the moment my beautiful little girl announced her arrival on the 29th of November 1990 with a massive wail. After a 5-hour, uncomfortable labour, I was handed a little bundle with ten tiny fingers, ten tiny toes and a shock of dark hair. So much hair! That would explain the heartburn, a midwife explained with a smile. All my pain melted away as I opened the little blanket to see this little helpless infant whose life depended on us. I breathed in her new baby smell, like an oxygen-starved drowning victim. I couldn't get enough of her little squirmy body, and all my built-up love spilled over for her.

Peter had driven me to the hospital as my labour started, dropped me off and went back to his mother's house.

Twice, as my labour progressed fast, the midwife asked me where my husband was. I had no idea. I naively assumed he was in the waiting room, as I thought he refused to be in the delivery ward, as according to him, "That should be no place for men, it's a woman's space."

But no, he was contacted by the reception nurse when she phoned the house phone number and spoke to his mother.

"Hy's net hier, wag 'n bietjie asseblief" *He's right here, just wait a moment please.*

The nurse obviously had some clout, which spurred him to get back to the hospital immediately. He strolled in as the baby was crowning and I was gripping a nurse's hand, eyes bulging and breathing hard. I didn't so much look at him, the midwife ignored him as I pushed my baby girl into the world with a cry. A quick jab of pethidine was all I was given.

"Oh, how wonderful, congratulations on your baby girl," the midwife beamed. I fell back exhausted and was relieved the pain was over as I opened the little blanket to inspect the little bundle, the most hurtful words stung like acid in a wound.

"It's a girl? Really? I'm sorry it's not a boy. I said I wanted a boy. Why has it got black hair? I KNEW IT, you fucking bitch, it's not mine! Who's is it?" The nurse was horrified, and he was asked to leave the room in disgust. I began to weep. I'd done it again, upset him over something opposite to what he wanted. I was too exhausted and upset to care at that point, and as the baby was wrapped up and taken to the nursery, I fell into a deep, fatigued, fitful sleep.

The Doctor informed me that my hospital admission would continue for at least a week, due to my labour and birthing coming quickly and the need for stitches. I just did as I was told. I thanked him, and I secretly gave thanks for being stitched up despite the uncomfortable sutures. I was allowed guests, and on the second day, in walked my only visitors – my parents. I remember Weff bursting into tears, and Dad had a brave, encouraging smile on his face. "Isn't she clever Dave, our little Zeb?" Looking over at the crib next to my bed, she scooped up her firstborn Granddaughter with tears in her eyes. Dad was holding in his emotions, something he'd learnt to control in the army years before. He put his arms around me, kissed my forehead, and asked me how I was.

This was my chance, which I could have spoiled everything. But stubbornness and hurt returned with added embarrassment and shame. I wasn't about to ruin this moment for them and me. What I don't tell them won't hurt them. I've made my bed and now I need to suck it up.

"I'm fine, honestly. Just tired. I'm so pleased you came to see me, though. How did you know?"

"The hospital called to say we have a little granddaughter and that you can have visitors."

My heart wanted so badly to burst open and let the floodgates out. But I didn't. I just couldn't.

> **FACT**
>
> "Over time, the mind of someone silenced in an abusive relationship can erode. Their sense of self-worth, autonomy, and confidence deteriorates. They may become anxious, depressed, or develop symptoms of PTSD. The longer they are silenced, the more the narcissist's control takes root, making it harder for them to see a way out. They use charm, lies, and manipulation to make the victim believe that they are dependent on the abuser for love, stability, or happiness."
>
> https://narcissistabusesupport.com/trapped-in-silence-how-narcissists-control-and-isolate-their-victims/

"Absolutely not, you're not staying in for a week. You've got to come home. New mothers don't need that long in the hospital. My mother never stayed in that long; there's nothing wrong with you, so why can't you come home? Make the Dr. agree to let you out, or I'll discharge you myself," he was hissing at me in a loud voice. Other new mothers were looking uncomfortable with the ruckus he was causing.

The next day, I was being driven home with our baby daughter in the back, having been discharged by force. I was tearful, sore, fearful, but already pouring with love for the little baby I'd just delivered.

As we arrived home, there had been some changes. Whilst I was in the Maternity Ward, Peter's mother had thankfully had us moved into the bigger bedroom in the house, to make room for our double bed and the cot, the wardrobe, and a dressing table. The furniture was half moved in already, but I was soon lifting and pushing the heavy bed and dressing table with Peter to position everything in place. I had been instructed by the nursing staff not to lift anything, to rest and ease myself in gently to get used to breastfeeding Tamara. Peter just laughed under his breath; told me it would be just fine, and I "wasn't an invalid."

Peter continued with his horse racing and gambling however, he had surprisingly landed a bit of a windfall. The house was getting crowded, it was noisy and cluttered, and tension brewed between father and son. They clashed, and there was a lot of animosity; you could cut the tension with a knife. So, it was decided that we needed to move.

There was a new housing development being built, and first-time buyer starter homes were being offered with an attractive mortgage deal. Crunching the numbers, we could just about afford the monthly repayments with the required "no deposit" attraction. It was across town, closer to Peter's job and further away from the rest of the family. I dared to live in hope that this just might be it – a new start to kickstart our future, a little family of 3. Sadly, it seemed I was still incapable of learning.

We moved into our newly built starter home and started our life as a family of 3. I had turned 20 and got into a routine as a devoted new Mum, feeding, nappy changes, washing, cleaning, cooking, and shopping on repeat. Even though we were living on our own now, do not think for one minute I was allowed to go anywhere on my own. Oh no, visitors were off limits too. Rules were increased and enforced.

Once in an absolute rage, Peter went through my wardrobe and tossed all my trousers into a heap. With adrenaline pumping through his body, with his bare hands, he tore my denim jeans in half right up the middle of the crotch. This was so that I didn't show off my "bits" in public.

Makeup and perfume were banned, or it'd be assumed I was attempting to get someone's attention.

If I needed to do grocery shopping, I had to take his mother or siblings with me so they could report back as usual.

Every morning and evening, he'd take the speedometer readings of the distance travelled so that I couldn't go anywhere without him knowing.

Grocery money was counted to the cent. After every shop, it was expected that I'd hand over the receipt to him so he could account for every penny spent.

He'd sneakily count the mugs or cutlery in the sink to see if anyone else had been around without him knowing, hoping to catch me out.

> **FACT**
>
> "Over time, you end up walking on eggshells. This results in post-traumatic stress disorder and anxiety. There are many examples of these arbitrary rules. They can apply to any aspect of your life. Many of them have to do with how you dress.
>
> Maybe your narcissist doesn't want you wearing something too sexy or not sexy enough. Maybe he/she doesn't want you wearing sweats or flip flops. It can be anything, the colour blue. Oftentimes, they seem hell bent on controlling what and how you eat as well, making comments such as, why are you eating that? In addition, they don't like how you move or talk or spend your time, and want to micromanage every aspect of your life."
>
> https://www.bustle.com/wellness/signs-you-are-experiencing-trauma-after-a-toxic-relationship

On the days he took the car to work instead of getting a lift from a colleague, he'd lock me in the house with Tamara. No concern over our safety if an emergency happened, this was so that he knew where I was whilst he was out. It goes without saying that I wasn't allowed my own set of house keys; he kept the only set.

I remember every time I heard his car pull up in the driveway, I would brace myself. I would look around the house quickly to see what he could possibly be angry about. I would run through the day's events in my mind to see if anything I'd done could have set him off. I would think back to our last conversation and try to remember if I would have to explain what I meant when I said whatever I said. I was on the defensive every time he came home. The sound of his car made me sick to my stomach, because I knew I had to react to however he acted – and I never knew how he was going to act.

The fear was real, and an hour before he was due home, my stomach would be churning and twisting with anxiety and dread.

Gaslit, manipulated, lied to, used, devalued, conditioned, controlled, and brainwashed.

One particular memory jumps out. I was expected to have a hot meal on a plate the moment he walked in from work – so this is what I obligingly did. Once he'd "ordered" his meal before he left that morning, he'd informed me exactly how he wanted his food cooked. Playing the dutiful wife, I had it planned and made his meal to the T, just the way he asked for it.

The way he arrived home in the driveway that night, I bristled. That sounded like I needed to be on alert, stay out of his way. The car came to a skid just outside the front door.

True to form, he burst through the door, smelling of oil. He'd had a hard, messy day, and he was tired. He walked straight past me to the bathroom, and I breathed a sigh of relief as he ignored me. He changed into shorts and a T-shirt and came and sat down to eat. He looked at the plate, then at me, back to the plate, back to me. He didn't utter a word, but picked up the plate of meat, veg and gravy and threw it as hard as he could across the kitchen like a Frisbee. The plate disintegrated on impact, splattering food all up the wall, ceiling, and floor.

"Wat die fok is die?" *What the fuck is this?* "Clean that shit up, you lazy bitch. Now, thanks to you, I'm starving and I'll have to go and find something to eat. I'm going to my Ma's (*mother's*), don't wait up."

He stormed out, locked the door as I fell to my knees with hot, heavy tears splashing in the gravy mess on the floor. What had I done wrong? It was exactly as he wanted it, the way he said he'd do it if he were cooking it. They were the vegetables he wanted, meat cooked exactly as he instructed, in his usual place at the breakfast nook. I couldn't fathom how I had cocked it up yet again. I wracked my brains as I swept up the broken bits but I was too scared to second-guess why.

Turns out I had dished it up on the wrong plate. Not the one he expected or wanted it on.

When you're an addict, there are very few people who can go cold turkey and switch off the desire for "just one more hit"

The same can be said for compulsive gamblers. For the few months we played house, bills were paid on time or a little late. We tried our best to keep the wolves at bay, but soon the demands and final notices were not enough, and our utilities were cut off. The phone line was cut off without warning.

Our lounge suite, which we had bought on hire purchase, became overdue. The TV Peter had taken a monthly hire contract for went into arrears. He pawned the loan TV to place a bet on a dead certainty, which he lost, and the loan sharks came a-knockin. We were living off the bare necessities, and one month, Tamara ran out of her SMA milk powder for her bottles, and I crumbled. The more debt that was built, the more he gambled – it was a vicious circle.

His parents didn't have any money to lend him to take the pressure off, and he was like a cornered animal.

His parents had taken on a similar mortgage deal to us, in a new starter home, as had his younger sister and brother-in-law. Much to my horror, both families moved to the same housing development just a walk away from our house. So once again, I was surrounded by his spies or "flying monkeys" as they are known in the NPD world.

Because of the risk of our house being repossessed as the debts piled high and kept coming, in an act of complete desperation, he turned to my Dad. It must have nearly destroyed him to admit we needed help from Dad, but he went cap in hand to ask for help. He had nowhere else to turn.

Dad, Peter, and I sat down and painstakingly Dad extracted all our mounting debt, itemised it all, divided Peter's salary into sections and worked out a proposal of a reliable payment plan.

And then in an act of sheer salvation, Dad caught us up so all bills were current, costing him thousands of Rands.

This was the closest I'd ever come to confessing about how miserable I was, how abusive Peter was and that the world had "just eaten me alive and spat me back out. I just couldn't live like this any longer, but the disgrace, oh, the shame of it. But something held me back – yet again.

Dad told me that I shouldn't give up on a marriage after just 6 months, reassuring me that if we stuck to the payment plan, we'd stay on top of things. Of course, he was totally unaware of the environment in which I was just surviving.

The mortgage was paid, and the house was saved. By this point, Peter had been working at the same company for a decent length of time and had had several increases. His salary was decent enough to live off of. We could have made real progress hereon in, but I'd lost my spark and endurance long ago.

Then the slippage started again, and money went missing, gambled away as if thrown into the wind or down the toilet. We got into a heated argument, and he was full of the usual manipulation and abuse, gaslighting and coercion. But I had had so much of it now, I could take it. So, he tried another tactic to scare me, and scare me it did.

He grabbed a can of Doom, the killer insect spray and sprayed enough into a glass and drank it. I was beside myself, frantic and with Tamara on my hip, ran all the way to his sister's house for help. 999

was called, and Paramedics were dispatched. By the time his sister and I had run back to our house, he was slumped on the floor, blue in the face. Paramedics arrived, whisked him away to pump his stomach.

I was in shock, trembling as I'd never seen anything like it. I blamed myself, as I thought it must be my fault that I had driven him to such desperation. He came home a few hours later, went to lie down with the bedroom door closed. I slept in Tamara's nursery, curled up on the carpet next to her cot, with a towel covering me as a blanket. I never slept.

Life continued a rollercoaster of anxiety, abuse, trauma, silences and demands.

I turned 21, and my 21st celebration, which my folks had planned, was ruined by Peter, purposefully. He put a spanner in the works to change plans at the last minute, attempting to disrupt the arrangements. In fact, every special occasion I had, he went out of his way to spoil things for me, in some way or another. It was power control he had over me, and he used it with every advantage he got.

He'd fly into a blind rage, seething with loathing every time anyone remarked how much Tamara looked like me. She is my double, and he hated that with a passion because, of course, all the attention was elsewhere and not on him. Mind-blowing.

Tamara's 1st birthday was another event that he kicked off about. His senseless jealousy and possessiveness of me spread to his own family members. Neither of his brother-in-laws was not welcome at the party; his father was too preoccupied with the day's horse racing and whiskey to bother attending, which I was glad about. His brothers were allowed as they were still schoolkids.

Weff and Dad attended but didn't stay long; he made it too uncomfortable. Mostly, it was the mothers in his family who had babies and children who came to the party. Most of them I didn't really know, as of course, I wasn't allowed to socialise even with his family much. Peter hung about to make sure no one uninvited turned up. I was too busy preparing party food and cleaning up spilt mess to be concerned with him hovering in the background.

The day passed without incident, and the next day all went back to our normal, which I now know wasn't normal.

> **FACT**
>
> "Narcissists have an insatiable need for attention and validation. During special occasions, such as birthdays or holidays, the spotlight is not solely on them, which can trigger feelings of inadequacy and jealousy. To regain control and centre the attention on themselves, narcissists may resort to disruptive behaviour, such as creating drama or causing conflicts"
>
> https://www.judgeanthony.com/blog/signs-a-narcissist-wants-your-attention.

Debra (20) with Tamara (3 weeks old)

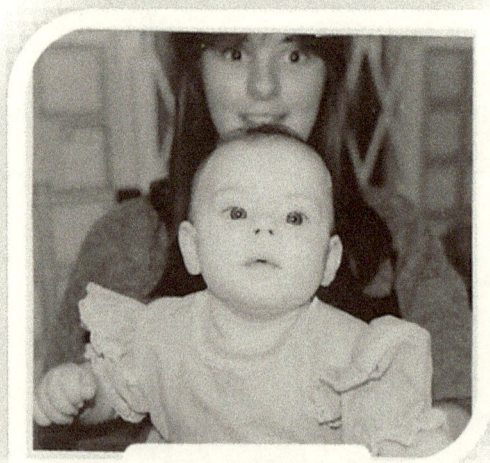
Debra (20) with Tamara (6 months old)

11
A LIFELINE WITH EMPTY PROMISES

> **FACT**
>
> "...and that's why we stay longer than we should...because it hurts to watch something you love transform into something you should hate. We sit and wait for it to return to its original state, in denial as we ignore the fact that what we see was always there and what is now, will always be."
>
> https://themindsjournal.com/and-that-s-why-we-stay-longer-than-we-should-2/

A couple of months after Tamara's birthday party, I kind of lost track a bit due to major trauma, shock, and distress. My brain won't unlock details that led up to the day it erupted like I'd never seen before.

That's what your brain does to protect itself. It locks moments of time and memories away that it thinks you wouldn't be able to cope with at the time, which is why Counselling and Trauma Therapy are essential for healing.

Peter had lost some weight and looked drawn, with sunken cheeks, yellow, pasty skin, and clammy. He was jittery and edgy.

I didn't dare broach the subject of illness or even worse, drugs of some description. I just left it alone and tried to avoid poking the beast. The smallest thing would kick him off: Tamara crying, me coughing too loud, washing not done when he expected it to be, or a mere look. Bearing in mind, we'd never had a washing machine, I was doing our washing over the bath, scrubbing oily overalls until my fingers bled.

There was no money for disposables, Tamara had terry towelling nappies which needed to be disinfected, washed and scrubbed too. It was hard labour but needed doing, so I just got on and did it.

I can't recall what set him off this time, but I know I have never seen a human morph into a demon before, apart from what he'd subjected me to up till now. Have you ever witnessed someone's eyes go black? With such an intense rage, you recoil in horror, and you know something awful is going to happen, but you have no idea what. It's a waiting game. You hardly dare breathe. The only phrase that is comparable is a "ticking time bomb" and you're just waiting for the explosion.

And then it goes off as if in slow motion.

I must have blacked out at some point because when I came to, he was gone. I didn't know where, but I guessed at his mother's. I crawled into bed, Tamara crying in her cot. I didn't have the strength to see to her right then. She quietened and fell back to sleep. I didn't. I lay there in the dark, quiet, throbbing, hurting, too tired to even shed any more tears. I was done in. All dried up like a husk.

It must have been hours later when I heard him come in. I didn't move, I lay frozen stiff, like a mannequin. He didn't say a word, but climbed into bed next to me. He flung his arm over me, and I stiffened further, hardly daring to breathe. That was a tactic so that if I tried to get up, he'd wake up with me moving. I lay there all night, allowing my mind to wander further than I had let it go up to now.

I'm not proud of the fact that I wished with all my might that he just wouldn't wake up in the morning. I'd fantasise about a life of freedom and that I'd just be rid of him for good. I closed my eyes, but sleep did not come. That night, I wished he would just perish. I prayed him to death.

The next morning, my hopes and prayers were dashed as I felt him get off the bed and go into the bathroom. Without a word he got dressed for work, took one look at me and then spat the words, "don't be here when I get home, you piece of shit. Take your stuff and fuck off. You disgust me you good for nothing whore. I won't be held responsible what happens if you're here when I get back," and turned on his heel and slammed the door.

I was wracked with terror in case he changed his mind and came back straight away. I waited for the sound of the engine to die away and then crawled off the bed. It took everything I had to move my bruised and aching body, to gather basic clothes for Tamara and me and throw them into a suitcase. I made her some bottles, packed her pram full to the brim with all I could carry and strapped her in.

He had taken the car, and the home phone had been cut off yet again, so I had only one choice. I half ran, half walked to his mother's house to ask her if I could use the phone. I had no money to use the call box at the shops, I didn't know any of the neighbours to approach – so I hedged my bets and made my way in the hot sun up to his mother's house, balancing my suitcase on top of the pram hood. I'd already planned what I'd do if our car was outside her gate, but by the grace of God, it was nowhere to be seen.

I put my suitcase out of sight outside the gate, opened the gate, and pushed the pram up the driveway.

I knocked on the door. She could see something had changed in my demeanour and urgency. The look of terror on my face must have been horrific, because she let me in straight away. I asked if I could use the phone, and she nodded in the direction of the phone table.

I called Dad. All my stubbornness, shame, and embarrassment instantly evaporated.

He answered the phone and, through tears, all I said to him was...

"Can you come get me?"

"Is this it?"

"I'm done"

"Where are you?"

"At his mother's"

"I'm on my way"

I put down the phone, thanked his mother, said bye, and wheeled Tamara out of her house and out the gate. I picked up my suitcase and walked to the end of the road, where there was an open vlei field and sat down on my suitcase amongst the waist-high grass. In a mixture of anxiety, nausea, heart palpitations, and sheer panic, I shrank into the grass every time a car passed, thinking it was Peter coming back. I hardly dare hope that this was actually happening.

Dad arrived in his bakkie pick-up truck, saw us, and stopped right in front of Tamara's pram. Without a word, he unbuckled Tamara and handed her to me, put her pushchair in the back, and I gratefully crawled into the cab beside him. No tears fell. I think I forgot how to cry.

He drove straight to our house, reassured me that it's all going to be ok, and to take what I needed for myself and Tamara. I packed more clothes, nappies, and a few toys, whilst Dad dismantled Tamara's cot. We packed the bakkie full with everything I knew that belonged to me, making sure to leave any of Peter's stuff, as I was not going to be accused of pilfering his paraphernalia. Besides, I wanted NOTHING from this monster.

"You are more powerful than you know, and they fear the day you discover it."

https://www.boldomatic.com

The first week back in my safety surroundings, it felt like I slept for a week, as well as going through the motions of being a new Mum, except I now had help. Positive help. Weff would help change nappies, and bathtimes were now fun. Dad loved feeding Tamara, cuddled on his lap in freshly washed pyjamas, and Lesley played endlessly with her, giving me a break. My family wrapped their arms around us both with loving, protective support. I'd forgotten what it felt like because the arms that I had been promised so easily, I had equally been so badly let down by.

For 6 weeks, I kept an open line of communication with Peter, but only gave updates about Tamara via phone calls to his mother. I didn't want to speak to him. I was too fearful of his voice, as it conjured up an ogre, a beast. I distinctly remember the first time his mother called me at Dad's house, my bladder just went, and I wet myself with fright. It was a trauma response.

Then he started with demands again, and I was petrified that he'd attempt custody proceedings, and I was determined to protect my beautiful little mini-me. I had to remain civil and co-operative and learn to put boundaries in place. With all the courage I had left in me, I agreed for him to come around to my parents' house to see Tamara, but I had the reinforcement of Dad being there, and there were rules…Dad's rules!

Thursday came, and he arrived after work and sat in the car outside the gate. He was not welcome on the property, so I went to the car with Tamara. She was 15 months old now. We sat in the car and talked. He really didn't look well, dishevelled, and thin. He was full of remorse and regret. Repentant and shamed, and begged me to reconsider returning home. He loved bombing the hell out of me, hoovered up and played on my fragile emotions, showered me with affection, attention, devotion, promises of counselling & guidance, and limited contact with his family as he could see now how toxic they were. He wanted to be a Dad that Tamara would be proud of, that we could achieve so much if we just worked together. That he had changed for the better and that he has seen the error of his ways. He'd had a recent promotion at work that had increased his salary, and he asked if we could start over, a fresh start? Would I be willing to give him a second chance, because surely everyone deserves one? Please? Give him one chance to prove that he's changed, and I wouldn't regret it. And if I changed my mind and wanted to come back to my parents, no questions asked – he'd bring me back straight away because I owed it to Tamara to let him be the Dad that he set out to be.

I had a discussion with my Dad about his proposal. He didn't want to know. Said it's my choice at the end of the day, but it's not just me I had to consider, and I had Tamara to think about now.

I mulled over Dad's words against the responsibility I now had, and how it would be all my fault that she could have a broken home, with weekend visits, split holidays, maintenance payments, and my mind went awol in a world I'd only read about as nobody in my family had ever been divorced. I couldn't bear it, and with a lump in my throat, I told Weff & Dad I would tolerate one more weekend with him.

Arriving back at the bare house, he had chatted all the way. Positiveness and reassurance seeped out of his bones as we pulled up in front of the garage. He carried Tamara into the house, and some of her toys were scattered about the living room. He helped me unpack, wrapped his arms around me tightly, kissed me and thanked me for giving him one last chance. "I've changed, I promise. I can't lose you both."

He made dinner, which was the first inkling of his change. He washed the dishes, and yes, the house was clean, had been freshly hoovered, and music was playing softly. That night, he was the gentle, attentive husband that I'd craved for so long, complimentary and bursting with love. We played with Tamara together, laughed and cried together, talked about plans, and put Tamara to bed together and then turned in ourselves.

He held me all night, whispering his apologies and begging for forgiveness. I reassured him I liked what I saw and that it was heading in the right direction. We snuggled together and were intimate once more, gentle, loving, soft, attentive. This side I had never seen, and I craved it.

We woke up the next morning, and he told me he needed to go out to run an errand. I stayed behind to see to Tamara, and whilst he was out, I looked around me. Everything looked tainted. It was like a sweet strawberry with a mouldy middle. Like a sidewalk chalk picture that had been rained on and smudged. Everything I looked at reminded me of the horrific time I had in the past.

And then I found it.

It was a little deliberately folded piece of paper squashed into a crevice in the kitchen. I pulled it out carefully and unravelled it. On it was written in Peter's handwriting, several Estcourt Agencies, Whore Houses, whatever you want to call them. Telephone numbers next to female names. I froze. When I gained my composure, I ran to the bathroom and threw up.

Peter came back and started making lunch. I told him I wasn't hungry, but I'd see to Tamara and pretended to fuss about her. I didn't make eye contact with him, but stiffened every time he came near me. I had to get out of there, somehow, without him cottoning on to what I had uncovered.

Mercifully, I'd forgotten some medication Tamara was meant to take, back at my parents' house. It was in the fridge and I'd forgotten all about it. I told Peter that Tamara couldn't be without it, so he agreed to drive us back to retrieve it. We got in the car and made the journey back.

Pulling up outside Weff and Dad's gate, I lifted Tamara out of the car, told him I'd be back shortly, and he sat in the car waiting. I went inside, shaking like a leaf. I had made my silent decision on the drive back over, convincing myself that it was all a ruse, all still about him. He'd absolutely crossed the ultimate line that I couldn't forgive. Without trust, we had nothing. Besides everything else he'd subjected me to.

Leaving Tamara in the capable hands of my parents inside, I walked back down the drive to face my fear. On that walk, something in me shifted, became stronger, sturdier, and calmer than I had felt in a long time. Deep breath, stay calm.

"I've decided we're not coming back with you. I just can't do it. I've made up my mind; nothing you can say will change my decision. That's it."

If I had slapped him hard, it wouldn't have changed the look on his face. It was something he was not used to, being stood up to. His brow furrowed, face darkened.

"But I've done everything I promised you I would. Why? Don't you want a future like we had planned? Please, I just want you and Tamara to come away with me for the weekend."

Something in the way he phrased that sentence turned me cold. Made all my arm hairs stand on end, and I felt that shift in me once again. Call it gut instinct, sixth sense, whatever you want, but something told me not to get into the car with him. Keep calm.

I refused and stood my ground, and began to watch the monster slowly reappear in him.

His final threat to me before he sped off was, "This is a Friday the 13th you'll NEVER forget."

He was right. I never have.

> ### FACT
>
> "Narcissistic rage is a malicious, out-of-control, and disproportionate type of anger that seeks revenge and destruction by any means possible.
>
> Lacking control threatens their sense of self and their grandiose façade, and their reaction to a perceived loss of control will be extreme."
>
> https://www.simplypsychology.org/when-a-narcissist-loses-control.html

I ran back up the driveway, phoned his mother to tell her he had just left my parents' house in a rage. Please could she check on him when he gets home, send one of his brothers or sisters down to the house and maybe stay the night. Just to ensure he had someone with him to make sure he was ok.
She promised she would.
She never did.

12
THE END AND NEW BEGINNINGS

> **FACT**
>
> "When a narcissist begins to lose control, there are clear and troubling behaviours that follow.
> Their collapse isn't just emotional—it's behavioural, and the actions they take during this time can have real consequences for those around them.
> Some of the most common signs that the narcissist in your life is on the brink of collapse are a sudden outburst, the silent retreat, acting out of desperation, emotionally harmful acts, and mental breakdown. One of the most significant triggers for a narcissistic collapse is exposure due to their mask slippage, revealing exactly who they are."
> https://narcissisticman.com/understanding-narcissism/narcissist-collapse/

The phone call came early the next morning. The call that released me from my tormented hell yet plagued me with guilt and has changed my world forever. Tamara's too.

Lesley answered the phone. She got me up out of bed and called me urgently to come to the phone. "It's Peter's mother."

I took the receiver and instantly felt fear grip me like a vice. I said "hello?" and all hell broke loose.

"He's followed through with it. You have killed him, Peter's dead." Her voice cracked and sobbed with grief, like only a mother could who has lost her child. "It's all your fault; you've done it this time."

My world spun, and I dropped the phone. I don't remember much after that—other than a few strange specific details. I remember Dad shouting "What??" and Weff running down the passage. I remember going tingly and numb and hearing Tamara babbling in the bedroom from her cot.

I remember Dad holding me as I collapsed onto the couch, my face in my hands, stunned with shock. And then the shakes started and wouldn't stop. Weff got me some sugar water followed by a mug of sweet tea. I was clearly in shock, unseeing, unfeeling, no tears, no words, nothing but frozen nothingness. It was only the second time in my life I'd seen Dad cry. Weff was as stunned, her eyes brimming for me.

How are you supposed to act when you've been conditioned and brainwashed to think and act unnaturally, devalued and injured by the person who has now caused such trauma to himself, to his own family, to his parents, who blame you, my family and then some?

How I coped, I could tell you not, because my brain has just locked up and won't go there even to this day. This I now know is the result of being in a permanent state of "fight, flight, freeze or fawn" for many years, combined with PTSD and severe anxiety.

But for certain, without the support of my saintly, caring parents and siblings, I wouldn't be here today pouring my heart out in this autobiography.

What hit me a few days later was that he had every intention of "taking Tamara and me AWAY with him that weekend," and the police later confirmed his intent. Chilling. If I had got into that car that Friday…we wouldn't be here today.

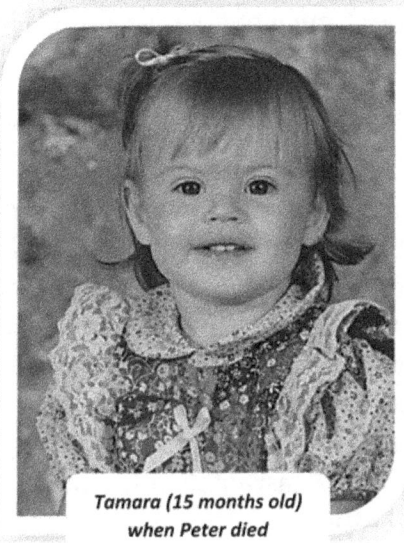

Tamara (15 months old) when Peter died

FACT

"The fight response is your body's way of facing any perceived threat aggressively. Flight means your body urges you to run from danger. Freeze is your body's inability to move or act against a threat. Fawn is your body's stress response to try to please someone to avoid conflict.

Whether you're in physical danger or psychological danger, your body will start triggering a stress response. This reaction starts in your amygdala, which is the section of your brain responsible for fear.

The amygdala transmits signals to your hypothalamus, stimulating the autonomic nervous system. Then, your sympathetic system stimulates your adrenal glands to trigger adrenaline and noradrenaline hormones."
https://www.webmd.com/mental-health/what-does-fight-flight-freeze-fawn-mean

The next weeks and months passed by in a daze, which I can only piece loosely together from what people close to me have shared. It felt like a huge prank somehow gone horribly wrong.

My Dad took charge of assembling all the details of what had transpired.

His mother had found him that morning in the closed garage with the car running. He'd gassed himself in our car with carbon monoxide from the exhaust fumes. Nobody had checked on him after I had called the day before to warn his mother that he had left in an insane rage. No one had kept an eye on him as requested. Thus, the state of mind he was in resulted in this. When his mother found him in the garage, the car door was open, engine still running, and he had fallen out of the car and in a last-ditch attempt to change his mind, attempted to crawl to the entrance. It seemed he hadn't the strength to lift the door up, and he lay with his arm outstretched toward the handle.

Peter's family refused to share any funeral details with me. It took Dad days ringing around the local funeral homes, hospitals, and mortuaries to find out where Peter was resting.

None of his family came forward to advise of the funeral details, except to inform me that I was banned from any service that would take place. His family didn't want to see me, hear me, or have me anywhere near them, nor Tamara.

Clearly, they had to find someone to blame for his untimely death, and they were laying the full blame of Peter's suicide at my feet, for if it weren't for me refusing to reunite with him (and be subjected to his ongoing abuse), he'd still be here.

Of course, nobody knew the extent to which Peter's behaviour and treatment of me had sunk, and I wasn't strong or brave enough to speak up for fear of the consequences I'd be subjected to. I had already been warned that nobody would believe me, so I needn't bother. Besides, the shame and embarrassment stopped any thoughts of confiding in anyone or asking for help.

Due to the immense shock of it all, Weff had taken me to our GP who had helpfully prescribed some sort of tranquilizers to tide me over in order to help me come to terms with the sudden trauma. I felt I was going to pieces.

A short time after, Dad presented me with all the details of the funeral and cemetery, where, how, what and when it was happening. He gently told me that if I wanted to go to the service which was scheduled for the next day, then it was my choice; however, he advised that I let it go ahead without me. Mentally and physically, I wasn't able to endure any more animosity and hostility, and I certainly wasn't about to create a scene, so I readily agreed. We agreed to take a drive to the cemetery much later, the same afternoon of the service, when everyone had left, so I could get some closure.

I repositioned some wreaths away and laid my cross of flowers on the head of his freshly dug burial place, and the tears dribbled out. Not with any remorse, but because it was expected of me. I was just going through the motions in a robotic state of mind.

I was waiting for him to sit up and accuse me of not crying hard enough, and why are the flowers white and not blue, and why am I wearing that, and where was his headstone proclaiming he was a loving, devoted husband and father? My trauma was palpable and very real. Slow breaths and I stayed calm.

The long arduous task of engaging a solicitor began, getting re-possession of my own house and car, dealing with all the debt as it all had to be reimbursed from his estate. There was so much that he got up to without my knowledge, cloak, and daggers, it all started revealing its ugly head.

There was much more debt than I realised, criminal activity and of course the infidelity and abuse.

As it turned out, when the authorities were called to the scene at the house the day of his death, Peter's mindless father told the authorities that Peter was unmarried, which is why I hadn't been contacted to verify information!

Apparently, according to a brother-in-law, at the graveside, Peter's father had to be restrained from falling onto the coffin as he was so inebriated.

The police granted me access back into my house, and it resembled a burglary. Belongings were strewn everywhere; the main bedroom was in a state. It was wholly obvious it had been rifled through prior to me regaining possession, and the only house keys which he had were now in the possession of his parents.

I went through the house, room by room, under the watchful, supportive eye of my Dad, propping me up each time I broke down, going through his things. I started making 2 piles of stuff: keeping and donating. The rest just got bagged up and went in the trash.

I didn't keep much: the rest of mine and Tamara's clothes, paperwork and the refrigerator, which was a wedding present bought with money gifted by my Grandad.

We found his suicide note specifically left for me to find, scribbled full of lies and accusations, pleading his love for Tamara and me, but also demanding yellow roses on his headstone.

It was about this time that we were contacted by Peter's older sister, the one who took an initial dislike to me. To this day, I have no knowledge of who informed her of what had really been going on in our relationship, or maybe she was part of those who went through the house afterwards and deduced it herself. But she had a sudden, dramatic change of heart and collected a few personal possessions she thought I might appreciate. His ID book, some photos, and his wedding ring, which he obviously was not wearing the day the police were in attendance.

Whilst packing my clothes, I pulled out his clothes from the cupboard and right at the back, purposely hidden, was a stockpile of prescription medication I'd never heard of, all prescribed to him. It was evident that he'd been stockpiling his meds without taking them – it could have accounted for his recent weight loss and ill look, sunken eyes and off-the-chart behaviour.

I bagged it up with the intention of taking it to the medical centre to ask some questions. Meeting with my doctor, it transpired that Peter was being treated for NPD (narcissistic personality disorder), BPD (borderline personality disorder), as well as schizophrenia. He was stunned that I had no knowledge of this, as he had been Peter's doctor since childhood. He'd also had several attempts at taking his own life prior to us even meeting, according to the physician, as he went through his medical history with us. Dad and I were dumbfounded. Yet more secrets are coming out of the woodwork.

And that wasn't all.

The despicable, most calculated shock was yet to be uncovered.

As a large company employed Peter, his employment contract stated he had a very good Death Benefit in Service, and that compensation for employees' spouses was x4 his final annual salary, and suicide was NOT an exclusion. I breathed a momentous sigh of relief. At least all the outstanding invoices and the solicitor would be uncovered.

Except when we submitted a claim to the Human Resources department, we were informed that Peter Carl Müller was an ex-employee and had resigned from his job 2 weeks before taking his life. Intentionally.

Yet again, he'd screwed me over in the worst way, but I didn't care about myself. He had taken away the chance of Tamara having a nest egg for her future. An education fund or for her first car. Unforgivable in my eyes. I hated him more than ever, and I felt bile and rage bubble up in my throat. I wanted in that moment to dig him up and kill him all over again!

It was then that I vowed I'd protect her from the world's horrors like my life depended on it. I was all she had. It was the day my life was put on hold, and my focus was all hers.

> **FACT**
>
> "Narcissists may derive a sense of satisfaction from hurting others, often as a means to assert their superiority and cope with their own insecurities.
>
> The self-centred tendencies of the person with narcissistic personality traits lead them, so we are told, to make rash decisions that ignore the hard facts.
>
> As a result, people high in narcissism may engage in risky behaviour such as gambling, spend money recklessly, and fail to take the more critical view that can benefit sober decision-making processes.
>
> Even though they may not live up to their own inflated expectations, they continue to see themselves as more capable and intelligent than others.
>
> We know, too, that narcissists have a vulnerable side. It's possible that their poorly-made decisions reflect a need to overcompensate for themselves as weak, incompetent, and flawed."
>
> https://www.understandnarcissism.com/post/schadenfreude-a-key-red-flag-of-narcissistic-personality

Another issue became evident when we discovered the car had been removed from the crime scene by his father. He'd gained possession of the car keys and had driven it to his own property. A family member had been using the car as a mode of transport to work. Of course, I knew nothing of it.

The car was on finance, and it formed part of the Estate. To regain custody of the car, we arranged a Police Escort to go with Dad and my brother to hand over the keys. I was spared being witness to that, but Andrew remembers it well.

Upon arrival at the home, the father answered the door to the police knock. And in his intoxicated state, Peter's father tried to argue with the office that he was keeping the car "in accordance with the police"

The policeman then sternly informed him, "Ons IS die Polisie, Meneer. Gaan haal vir my die sleutels nou asseblief" *We ARE the Police, Sir. Go and get the keys for me now, please.*

The car was acquired, resold, and was just about the only equity in the whole of this chaos.

Once the Estate had wrapped up, the best possible outcome from this dire disaster was that my house was re-possessed by the bank as Peter had not kept up the mortgage payments, and that included the lounge suite and any other furniture bought on HP. Most of the creditors wrote off the debt based on Peter's death. The equity in the Estate strangely resembled the amount Dad had previously forked out on the bills, and I relinquished it all to Dad. I owed him my life.

It was about this time I became ill, shivering, hot & cold, achy and crampy. I put it down to the flu. My period had started too and was exceptionally heavy. I returned to the Dr who prescribed analgesics for my symptoms, and said my body is probably reacting to the shock despite the tranquilizer medication he'd put me on.

I went home and tried to get on with daily life in a daze as best I could with my support once again around me.

I couldn't shake this virus or whatever was making me sick – until it suddenly dawned on me that I was miscarrying!!

Panic stricken, I confided in Weff and together we worked the dates back to the one single night I had returned with Peter to our house where he was being so very loving and caring. I fell for it hook, line, and sinker – manipulated and played to the very last.

Immediately Weff booked a Dr's appointment, who confirmed it and said it was almost probably due to the tranquilizers he'd prescribed me – he asked me if I knew I was pregnant at the time, to which I said I'd assumed not as we'd been split up for 6 weeks.

Stupidly I'd not thought about that night since finding his folded up bit of evidence – I just wanted to forget everything that was connected to Peter.

I would NEVER have coped with 2 very young babies on my own, so I think about it as a blessing in disguise under those circumstances.

My Mum arranged for a D&C to be booked, and on the day Dad drove me to the Park Lane Hospital for it to be carried out. Another end to this horrific saga.

Many months later, I was contacted by Peter's mother. They wanted to know if we were prepared to sit down and discuss a headstone, of course, it was all about the cost.

Initially, I thought after everything they'd put me through, I never wanted to clap eyes on any of them again. But Dad, in his wisdom, calmly made me see reason. I needed to be seen as co-operative and even if I didn't want a headstone, I had to think of Tamara for when she was older. She would at least have somewhere to go if she so wished, to piece together her heritage.

We arranged to meet with a stonemason, and I sat in stony silence. Listened calmly to what their proposal was, and of course, the family had already planned what they wanted. I was disregarded in the choosing, but I damn well made sure that it said, "wife Debra and daughter Tamara," with a spray of yellow roses engraved on it.

And I paid half the invoice.

I had racked up quite a track record in such a short space of time, which certainly was life teaching me a lesson with a sharp kick in the backside. Peter was 24 when he passed. I had been married for 2 and a half years of torment and misery. My only treasure was in the form of my beautiful little girl, for who's world was now my entire focal point and focus.

Married at 19, Mum at 20, Widow at 21.

Poignant and heartbreaking.

Yet here I was, as Dad had taught me, staying calm.

How much more could I endure? My life stretched out before me, not such a blank page now but like a rather crumpled road map, waiting to be smoothed out and tentatively discovered.

Little did I know how much more stronger I was going to have to be......life was about to get a whole lot harder.

SOMETIMES, YOU DON'T REALISE HOW TERRIBLE SOMEONE
TREATED YOU UNTIL YOU ARE EXPLAINING IT TO SOMEONE ELSE

♥

YOU DIDN'T QUIT ON HIM.
YOU SAVED YOURSELF. YOU FINALLY CHOSE YOURSELF AFTER A
LONG WHILE OF CHOOSING SOMEONE WHO REFUSED TO CHOOSE
YOU BACK.
BE PROUD OF THAT. IT TOOK STRENGTH, AND YOU HAVE NOTHING
TO FEEL BAD ABOUT. PLEASE, DON'T LET THEM GUILT TRIP YOU.
AND DON'T LET YOUR WILLINGNESS TO BE SO FORGIVING EVER
MAKE YOU SECOND GUESS YOUR DECISION.
IT WAS THE RIGHT ONE.

♥

ONE DAY YOU WILL TELL YOUR STORY OF HOW YOU HAVE
OVERCOME WHAT YOU WENT THROUGH, AND IT WILL BECOME
SOMEONE ELSE'S SURVIVAL GUIDE

ABOUT THE AUTHOR

DEBRA LINDSEY (nee TORRY), born in Rhodesia in 1970, has danced with darkness, wrestled with doubt, and somehow still managed to find redemption. Her journey through mental health challenges hasn't been linear—or particularly graceful—but it's been honest, raw, and deeply human.

From panic attacks to breakthrough moments, she's faced the kind of obstacles that don't come with a manual, only with determination, perseverance, and bravery.

This autobiography is a tribute to the love of her family, survival, self-discovery, and the messy beauty of healing. With vulnerability as her superpower and humour as her shield, Debra shares a story that proves strength isn't about never falling—it's about getting back up, again and again, with positivity and stubborn courage.

BREAKING FREE AND STAYING CALM

NARCISSISM AND NARCISSISTIC PERSONALITY DISORDER (NPD)

What is a Narcissist?
The definition of a narcissist, clinically speaking, refers to someone who meets the criteria for narcissistic personality disorder (NPD). It's a complex mental health condition that includes a deep need for admiration, a lack of empathy, and an inflated sense of self-importance. But even outside a formal diagnosis, narcissistic behaviours—like manipulation, entitlement, or emotional detachment—can still cause harm, especially in close relationships.

Spotting the signs of narcissism can help you make sense of confusing interactions and set healthier boundaries. Whether you're navigating a difficult relationship or trying to understand your own patterns, here's what to consider:

Narcissism and **NPD** represent different points on a spectrum of self-focused behaviour, but it's important to distinguish between the two.

Narcissism refers to characteristics that everyone exhibits to some degree, including confidence, self-assurance, and the ability to lead others.

On the other hand, NPD is a recognized mental health condition that involves a pattern of extreme and debilitating behaviour. People with NPD tend to have an inflated sense of their own importance, a deep need for excessive attention and admiration, and a lack of empathy.

The key difference between narcissism as a trait and NPD as a disorder lies in the intensity and consistency of the behaviours.

While typical narcissistic traits can be seen in many people without significant impact on their functionality or relationships, **NPD affects almost all areas of a person's life, impairing their ability to maintain healthy personal and professional relationships.**

While narcissism might relate to a particular context or occasion, the patterns seen in NPD are *persistent* and *pervasive* and often require professional intervention for improvement.

What is Emotional Manipulation in a Relationship?

Emotional manipulation is a form of emotional abuse where a manipulator uses subtle or deceptive tactics to affect another person's emotions, thoughts or behaviors, with the goal of gaining control. Gradually, it erodes trust in relationships and leads to feelings of anxiety, confusion, guilt, and self-doubt in the victims.

LoveLens Insights

15 Emotional Manipulation Tactics in a Relationship

1. They gaslight you
2. They exploit you
3. They triangulate you
4. They love-bomb you
5. They ghost you
6. Silent treatment
7. Projections
8. Name-calling
9. They backstab you
10. They joke when you're serious
11. They change the subject
12. They dismiss or ignore serious concerns
13. They guilt-trip you
14. They blame you for the abuse
15. They avoid accountability

LoveLens Insights

https://blog.calm.com/blog/what-is-a-narcissist
https://lovelensinsights.com/emotional-manipulation-tactics/

Overt vs. Covert Narcissists

Overt and covert narcissists represent two distinct expressions of narcissistic traits.

Overt narcissists, also known as grandiose narcissists, display obvious self-importance and seek admiration openly. They often dominate conversations and boast about their achievements.

Covert narcissists, in contrast, exhibit a more subtle form of narcissism. They may appear shy or self-deprecating on the surface. However, they harbor similar feelings of superiority and entitlement as their overt counterparts.

Key differences:

Overt narcissists: Extroverted, charismatic, openly arrogant

Covert narcissists: Introverted, sensitive to criticism, passive-aggressive

Both types struggle with empathy and maintain a fragile self-esteem beneath their outward behaviours.

Overt (Grandiose) Narcissist	Covert (Vulnerable) Narcissist
Presentation: Outwardly confident, bold, arrogant, and attention-seeking.	**Presentation:** Appears shy, self-deprecating, or passive-aggressive, flying under the radar.
Behavior: Directly manipulates, demands, and may become aggressive when challenged.	**Behavior:** Uses subtle manipulation, passive-aggression, and may be hypersensitive to criticism.
Grandiosity: Expresses their inflated sense of self-importance openly and directly.	**Grandiosity:** Internalizes their sense of superiority, often seeking attention through feigned humility or by playing the victim.
Vulnerability: May hide their insecurities behind a tough, confident exterior.	**Vulnerability:** Often exhibits more outward signs of anxiety, depression, and a chronic need for reassurance.

Key Similarities

Core Traits: Both share an inflated sense of self-importance and a deep-seated need for admiration and validation.

Lack of Empathy: A fundamental lack of empathy is present in both types.

Fragile Self-Esteem: Both types have a fragile sense of self-worth that fuels their manipulative behaviors.

How They Differ in Practice

Perception: You might immediately feel an overt narcissist's traits upon meeting them, while a covert narcissist's traits can remain hidden for years.

Manipulation: Overt narcissists use direct methods like bullying and demands, whereas covert narcissists employ more subtle tactics like gaslighting, passive-aggression, and creating pity to get their needs met.

Attention: Overt narcissists demand the spotlight, while covert narcissists seek attention by constantly seeking reassurance and attention for their perceived misfortunes or talents.

Primary expressions

Two primary expressions of narcissism have been identified: **grandiose** ("thick-skinned") and **vulnerable** ("thin-skinned"). Recent accounts post that the core of narcissism is self-centred antagonism (or "entitled self-importance"), namely ***selfishness, entitlement, lack of empathy, and devaluation of others***.

Grandiosity and vulnerability are seen as different expressions of this antagonistic core, arising from individual differences in the strength of the approach and avoidance motivational systems. Some researchers have posted that genuine narcissists may fall into the vulnerable narcissism subtype, whereas grandiose narcissism might be a form of psychopathy.

Grandiose narcissism

Narcissistic grandiosity is thought to arise from a combination of the antagonistic core with temperamental boldness—defined by positive emotionality, social dominance, reward-seeking and risk-taking. Grandiosity is defined—in addition to antagonism—by a confident, exhibitionistic, and manipulative self-regulatory style:

High self-esteem and a clear sense of uniqueness and superiority, with fantasies of success and power, and lofty ambitions.

Social potency, marked by exhibitionistic, authoritative, charismatic and self-promoting interpersonal behaviours.

Exploitative, self-serving relational dynamics; short-term relationship transactions defined by manipulation and privileging of personal gain over other benefits of socialization.

Vulnerable narcissism

Narcissistic vulnerability is thought to arise from a combination of the antagonistic core with temperamental reactivity—defined by negative emotionality, social avoidance, passivity and marked proneness to rage. Vulnerability is defined—in addition to antagonism—by a shy, vindictive and needy self-regulatory style:

Low and contingent self-esteem, unstable and unclear sense of self, and resentment of others' success

Social withdrawal, resulting from shame, distrust of others' intentions, and concerns over being accepted

Needy, obsessive relational dynamics; long-term relationship transactions defined by an excessive need for admiration, approval and support, and vengefulness when needs are unmet.

Sexual

Sexual narcissism has been described as an egocentric pattern of sexual behaviour that involves an inflated sense of sexual ability or sexual entitlement, sometimes in the form of extramarital affairs. This can be overcompensation for low self-esteem or an inability to sustain true intimacy.

While this behavioural pattern is believed to be more common in men than in women, it occurs in both males and females who compensate for feelings of sexual inadequacy by becoming overly proud or obsessed with their masculinity or femininity.

The controversial condition referred to as "sexual addiction" is believed by some experts to be sexual narcissism or sexual compulsivity, rather than an addictive behaviour.

Narcissistic Parents

Narcissistic parents often see their children as extensions of themselves and encourage the children to act in ways that support the parents' emotional and self-esteem needs. Due to their vulnerability, children may be significantly affected by this behaviour. To meet the parents' needs, the child may sacrifice their own wants and feelings. A child subjected to this type of parenting may struggle in adulthood with their intimate relationships.

In extreme situations, this parenting style can result in estranged relationships with the children, coupled with feelings of resentment, and in some cases, self-destructive tendencies.

Origins of narcissism in children can often come from the social learning theory. The social learning theory proposes that social behaviour is learned by observing and imitating others' behaviour. This suggests that children are anticipated to grow up to be narcissistic when their parents overvalue them.

Narcissism in the workplace

There is a compulsion among some professionals to constantly assert their competence, even when they are wrong. Professional narcissism can lead otherwise capable and even exceptional professionals to fall into narcissistic traps. "Most professionals work on cultivating a self that exudes authority, control, knowledge, competence and respectability. It's the narcissist in us all—we dread appearing stupid or incompetent."

Executives are often provided with potential narcissistic triggers. Inanimate triggers include status symbols like company cars, company-issued smartphones, or prestigious offices with window views; animate triggers include flattery and attention from colleagues and subordinates.

Narcissism has been linked to a range of potential leadership problems, ranging from poor motivational skills to risky decision-making, and in extreme cases, white-collar crime.

High-profile corporate leaders who place an extreme emphasis on profits may yield positive short-term benefits for their organisations, but ultimately drag down individual employees as well as entire companies.

Narcissism can also create problems in the general workforce. For example, individuals high in narcissism inventories are more likely to engage in counterproductive behaviour that harms organisations or other people in the workplace. Aggressive (and counterproductive) behaviours tend to surface when self-esteem is threatened.

Individuals high in narcissism have fragile self-esteem and are easily threatened. One study found that employees who are high in narcissism are more likely to perceive the behaviours of others in the workplace as abusive and threatening than individuals who are low in narcissism.

Relationships

Narcissism can have a profound impact on both personal and professional relationships, often creating toxic dynamics. In romantic relationships, narcissistic individuals **typically demand attention and admiration from their partner while offering little in return**. They often **fail to show empathy or concern** for their partner's emotional needs, focusing instead on fulfilling their own desires.

The narcissist's **behaviour can shift dramatically, alternating between idealising their partner—viewing them as perfect—and devaluing them when the narcissist no longer feels validated.** This inconsistency can cause emotional confusion and distress for the partner, leaving them feeling undervalued and emotionally drained.

Celebrity

Celebrity narcissism (sometimes referred to as acquired situational narcissism) is a form of narcissism that develops in late adolescence or adulthood, brought on by wealth, fame and the other trappings of celebrity. Celebrity narcissism develops after childhood and is triggered and supported by the celebrity-obsessed society. Fans, assistants and tabloid media all play into the idea that the person really is vastly more important than other people, triggering a narcissistic problem that might have been only a tendency, or latent, and helping it to become a full-blown personality disorder. "Robert Millman says that what happens to celebrities is that they get so used to people looking at them that they stop looking back at other people." In its most extreme presentation and symptoms, it is indistinguishable from narcissistic personality disorder, differing only in its late onset and its environmental support by large numbers of fans. "The lack of social norms, controls, and of people centring them makes these people believe they're invulnerable", so that the person may suffer from unstable relationships, substance abuse or erratic behaviours.

Social media

Social media has played a significant role in shaping and amplifying narcissistic behaviours in recent years. Platforms such as Instagram and TikTok encourage users to share content that emphasises their personal achievements and appearance, often rewarding those who gain the most likes and followers. Narcissistic individuals are more likely to use these platforms for self-promotion and validation. The trend of posting selfies and curated images is particularly prevalent among individuals who seek external approval to boost their self-esteem. The constant feedback from social media algorithms, which prioritise highly engaging content, further fuels narcissistic tendencies. While this can lead to increased attention and admiration, it can also create emotional instability. Narcissists often experience negative feelings, such as anxiety or depression, when they do not receive the validation they expect. This pressure to maintain an idealised online persona can lead to emotional distress, especially when their real-world interactions do not match the image they present online.

Destructive narcissism is the constant exhibition of a few of the intense characteristics usually associated with pathological narcissistic personality disorder, such as a "pervasive pattern of grandiosity", which is characterised by feelings of *entitlement and superiority, arrogant or haughty behaviours*, and a generalised *lack of empathy and concern for others*.

On a spectrum, destructive narcissism is more extreme than healthy narcissism but not as extreme as the pathological condition.

Pathological levels of narcissism

Extremely high levels of narcissistic behaviour are considered pathological.

It manifests itself in the *inability to love others, lack of empathy, emptiness, boredom, and an unremitting need to search for power*, while making the person unavailable to others. The clinical theorists

Kernberg, Kohut, and Theodore Millon all saw pathological narcissism as a possible outcome in response to *unempathetic and inconsistent early childhood interactions*. They suggested that narcissists try to compensate in adult relationships.

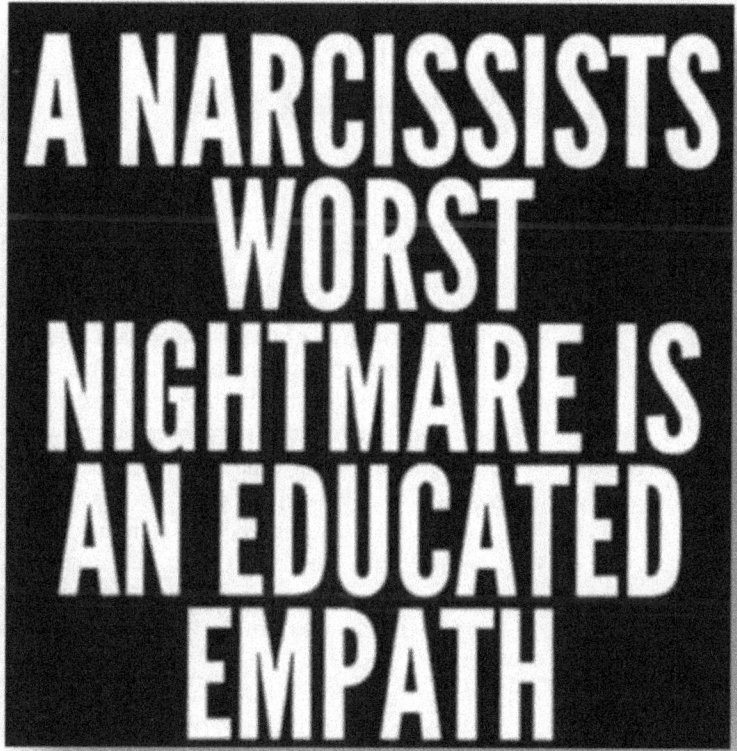

https://en.wikipedia.org/wiki/Narcissism#Expressions_of_narcissism

WARNINGS
Behaviours to be aware of

PHRASE	DESCRIPTION
Achievement Robbers	Their combination of laziness and entitlement, and given the charade of the false self, you will find that they are great at claiming other people's hard work and success as theirs. These are the bosses who are hard taskmasters to their subordinates, whilst too busy brown-nosing their seniors and wining and dining clients to roll up their sleeves themselves. These are the spouses who skip on household chores because they are too busy somewhere else, anywhere else. These are the partners who bum all day and expect their other halves to bring home the bacon.
Addictions	Narcopaths get easily bored with the mundane and are natural risk-takers. They will often have addictions (drink, drugs, sex, gambling, etc) as well as to drama and adrenaline.
Big Ego	This is the hallmark of the overt narcissist – brash, full of their own achievements, dismissive of other people, dismissive of the failures, unaccountable for their cock-ups, vain and overly pre-occupied with their image. Many will be able to see politicians and celebs falling into these stereotypes. But beware, whilst this may be a key giveaway for the overt narcissists, there are many of other types of narcissists who do not fit this mould. Even with the covert ones, though, once you get to know them intimately, you'll have this overwhelming feeling that in their lives, it's all about them.

PHRASE	DESCRIPTION
Blackmail	Emotional blackmail involves using fear, obligation, or guilt to manipulate others into compliance. Narcissists might threaten self-harm or abandonment to get their way.
Breadcrumbing	Where the narcissist gives small amounts of affection and attention to their victim to keep them hooked and hanging out for more.
Centre of Attention	Narcopaths adore being the centre of attention and resent attentiveness being lavished on anyone else – particularly members of the same sex. Their favourite topic of conversation is, you've guessed it, themselves. They will try and sit in the middle of a large dinner table, they will be the first to dance on tables, and expect loud high spirits at parties.
Co-dependency	Co-dependency is essentially where someone seeks safety, security, survival and love outside of themselves, rather than learning to meet those needs themselves. People who have grown up or lived in abusive or unstable environments tend to become codependent as a result of the abuse. They are programmed that their needs don't matter and the needs of the other person must always come first.
Coercive Control	Coercive control is where an abuser uses non-physical tactics to control their victim through fear. They will gaslight, manipulate, stonewall, isolate, intimidate and threaten as a means to program their victim. The idea is to instil fear in the victim to get them to do what they want, rather than raising a hand. Coercive control is a very sly and insidious abusive technique, which is often used by narcissists.
Cognitive Dissonance	Where the mind has two opposing thoughts or beliefs at the same time, it's essentially a psychological state that keeps you clinging to who you think the narcissist is, rather than who they truly are. One day they're loving, the next they're cruel and rageful. This abuse pattern keeps you in a state of confusion and self-doubt, losing the ability to trust your own judgment.

PHRASE	DESCRIPTION
Controlling	They must control situations, and particularly their partner and children, household finances, social engagements, and family plans. Only those whom they can confidently control are allowed into their core circle of friends. Those who demonstrate critical thinking and an independent mind are kept at a distance. In the workplace, they will often control subordinates ruthlessly.
Dysfunctional Relationship with their Kids	If they have kids from a previous relationship, expect the relationship with the kids, or between the kids and their other parent, to be dysfunctional – they have either sole custody or very little contact with their kids. Again, either way, it will be the fault of the kids' other parent.
Emotional and Psychological Abuse	Narcissists often engage in verbal abuse, using insults, criticism, and humiliation to erode their victim's self-esteem. They may alternate between praise and criticism to keep others dependent on their approval.
Enabler	An enabler is someone who allows the narcissist's behaviour. They perpetuate the abusive behaviour out of fear of the narcissist's reactions (survival) or because it's been so normalised in their world that they can't see that there's anything wrong with it.
Entitled	They have a sense of entitlement – to borrow money or things, to preferential treatment, to adoration.
Exploitative	They are personally exploitative of others. Nothing is done out of generosity, although generous deeds may be done for show.
Fawning	The fawn response in abuse victims is where they abandon their own needs in order to tend to the abuser and avoid conflict or punishment.
Financial Abuse	Narcissists may also use financial abuse to maintain control, restricting access to money or creating economic dependence.

PHRASE	DESCRIPTION
Flying Monkeys	Narcissists have an uncanny ability to get through to you, even when you've made an effort to create some distance between you and them. To sidestep any communication boundaries you've set, they'll often employ a third party — a friend you have in common, your sibling or other parent if it's your mom or dad that you're dealing with, or a fellow coworker if your narc is in the workplace. Flying monkeys describe the people in the narcissist's life whom they enlist to do their dirty work for them.
Gaslighting	This is a prevalent tactic used by narcissists to make others question their perception of events. They may deny saying or doing things, even in the face of clear evidence.
Good Listener	Don't mistake this one for the warm and kind style of listening and empathising – the narcissist's form of listening is more intent on studying. From the outset, narcs are looking for opportunities to get their hooks into you, signs of weakness, an indication of the tank of narcissistic fuel you represent, what makes you tick, etc.
Grey Rock	To go 'grey rock' is where you take on the energy of the most boring, forgettable grey rock you can imagine. You don't enable the narcissist or react to them in any way, and basically be so boring that the narcissist will lose interest and move on to another target.
Haughty Attitude	Whilst they might be trying to impress you and conduct themselves accordingly, they nevertheless appear to have a very haughty demeanour, particularly to people like restaurant waiting staff. Look for self-importance, pomposity, rudeness, and a self-aggrandising attitude.
Hoover	Hoovering is a common tactic that narcissists will use when you have escaped (or are escaping) their toxic web and they want to pull you back into their world. The aim of hoovering is to coerce a person, through seemingly innocent and kind gestures, back into a position where the narcissist can use them for their own personal gain.

PHRASE	DESCRIPTION
Lack of Object Constancy	Like the chameleon, narcs will tailor themselves to best shine depending on the company or situation they are in. Invariably, they will treat their nearest and dearest differently behind closed doors. So whether it's their political persuasion, hobbies, interests, favourite food or colour – expect things to change whenever the wind blows.
Lack of sincere apologies	Narcopaths struggle to apologise, genuinely, for anything. They just can't be wrong – admitting it dents their sense of perfect "false self". They will either freeze, change the subject or otherwise dodge, or mumble an apology followed with a "but….".
Lacking Empathy	They cannot feel emotions such as love, empathy, remorse, compassion – although they are expert at feigning them, having studied others carefully.
Lazy	Narcs are fundamentally lazy. Look carefully and you will see that they are the last to volunteer for anything menial or arduous. Unless there is narcissistic supply to be had, don't expect them at many selfless events.
Love bombing	Expect plenty of compliments, frequent texts and messages professing undying love and attraction. Right from the get-go, they want to dominate your thoughts on an hourly basis. This serves a secondary role – you're not developing an interest in anyone else. Messages may seem rather generic, and not necessarily tailored to you specifically – and that's because they are not genuine or original, but copied from films, books and the like..
Low respect for Rules and the Law	Their lack of empathy for individuals extends to wider society – they just don't care about anyone else. Add to this their appetite for risk, their pathological lies and their sense of entitlement, and you will understand why an estimated 25% of the prison population have NPD.

PHRASE	DESCRIPTION
Mirroring	Narcissists position themselves as being your soulmate by mirroring. In the early days, anticipate plenty of in-depth questions as they get to know you. Getting to know one-another is normal in a relationship, but with a narcissist, it is more of a study, and it's very one-sided. They won't want to give anything away until you have first disclosed. Then they will pretend to like all of the same things as you – hobbies, past-times, sports, interests, music, food, places to visit, drink, etc..
Narcissist's Mask	The narcissist's mask is the facade of their False Self. It's the image they portray for how they want to be seen, rather than who they truly are. The narcissist's mask is what they use to manipulate people into handing over narcissistic supply.
Narcissistic FOG	Acronym for 'Fear, Obligation and Guilt.' Narcissists use these tactics to keep their victims in a fog and unable to see what's really going on behind their manipulations.
Narcissistic Rage	Narcissistic rages are often caused by a deep inner trauma being triggered within the narcissist. However, the narcissist does not want to feel those things, so they push all of their emotions outward in a big ball of anger. And now it's all your fault! Narcissistic rages can be terrifying to witness and can sometimes turn violent. Narcissists use rage to control those around them through fear, while completely disowning the parts of themselves they don't like and dumping them onto you.
Narcissistic Supply	Narcissistic supply refers to the attention, admiration, and validation that narcissists crave. It fuels their inflated sense of self-importance. It is the life force energy narcissists require to abate their empty black hole, which is filled with utter shame, self-loathing and disgust. Narcissists need 'supply' for their psychological survival.

PHRASE	DESCRIPTION
No Contact	No contact is where a victim of narcissistic abuse chooses to sever all ties with the narcissist due to having their boundaries systematically broken over and over again. This is where all attempts of contact by the narcissist are denied and the victim completely blocks the narcissist at their end. Oftentimes, going no contact with a narcissist is the only way to free yourself from their abusive cycle and be able to heal healthily.
Overly Sexual	Whilst they may not be able to feel love, sexual conquest represents validation, and therefore narcissistic supply, to the narc. So expect them to be sexual before your level of intimacy has built commensurately.
Plenty of Charm	They know how to win people over quickly and will come across very charming – but only to those people who 'count'. Expect the vicar to be treated very differently to the rubbish collector. The charm is false, however – something that their "false selves" use to give the impression of a nice person, a pillar of society. Their intimate partners are the only ones really to see their charming sides in public – in private, give up hope now.
Plenty of Crazies	Narcs leave a wake of destruction in their paths. But they themselves cannot be accountable for this situation – so it must be their victims, right? Look out for the narc dismissing their exes, etc as crazy or having a screw loose. And often abusive – they are masters at projecting their own faults onto their victims.
Projection	Narcopaths are masters of projection – blaming others for exactly those traits they are guilty of themselves. Projection involves attributing their own negative traits or behaviours to others. This allows narcissists to avoid taking responsibility for their actions..

PHRASE	DESCRIPTION
Quick with Intimacy	Normal range people allow time for their feelings to develop – and these emotions come naturally. Less so with the Narcissist, who has simply cannot feel emotions around intimacy. They are on a mission to derive supply, and get rather impatient with normal-range targets taking their time.
Red Flags	Red flags are warning signs throughout the relationship that suggest things aren't quite right. People with low boundary function and co-dependency often ignore or miss red flags due to the overwhelming desire for the narcissist (or other person) to be who they really want them to be.
Silent Treatment	The silent treatment is a form of emotional manipulation where narcissists withdraw communication to punish or control others. This can be deeply distressing for the recipient.
Smear Campaign	Narcissists will embark on smear campaigns when they want to control the public storyline to suit their agenda. They will drag your good name through the mud with the intent of totally ruining you. Everything with a narcissist is about winning. So, if they can't control you or what you're saying about them, they'll do everything they can to completely annihilate you. They must do this to keep their false image intact. You see, you know too much about them now, and they cannot risk you telling anyone about who they truly are behind their mask.
Stonewalling	The refusal to communicate with someone. A common tactic used by a narcissist to actively block the connection by being evasive, refusing to answer any questions and not cooperating with any attempts at contact. The famous narcissistic silent treatment is a great example of stonewalling. They use it to intentionally put their victim into a state of anxiety and hold out with the 'reward' (granting of communication) to control them.

PHRASE	DESCRIPTION
Trauma Bonding	Trauma bonding often occurs, causing victims to feel attached to their abusers despite the harm. The victim feels bonded to the person who's destroying them because they feel the abuser is the only person who can provide them with the relief they so desperately seek to abate their intense anxiety.
Triangulation	Triangulation creates conflict between two parties, with the narcissist positioning themselves as the mediator or victim. This tactic divides and conquers, keeping others off-balance.
Word Salad	The purpose of a word salad is to create mass confusion in a conversation and take the other person down such an elaborate rabbit warren of topics that you can't even remember where the conversation began. Narcissists are masters at using word salad as a manipulation tactic, which serves to distract the other person away from any truth or blame towards the narc.
You're Treading on Eggshells	In normal friendships and relationships, your bond should be strong enough to feel confident that you could disagree or tell them some home truths. With a Narcopath, you may sense an unwritten rule, a gut feeling, that you don't challenge them. Ever. Moreover, they can often ooze a mood that they are angry and on the verge of an explosion, so you must tread carefully.

https://narcopath.info/about-npd/overview/red-flags-of-narcissism/
https://unmaskingthenarc.com/glossary-of-narcissistic-abuse-terms/

Narcissistic relationships follow a predictable cycle of idealisation, devaluation, and discard.

These stages create an emotionally turbulent dynamic that can be damaging to the non-narcissistic partner, often leaving targets confused and traumatised.

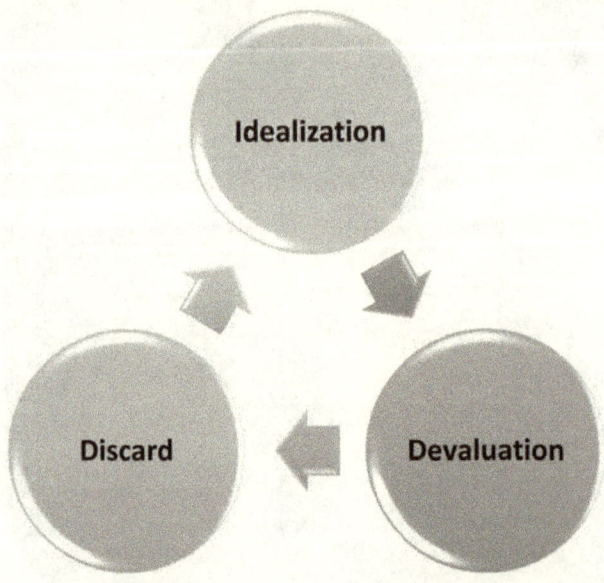

Idealization Phase

The idealisation phase marks the beginning of a narcissistic relationship. During this stage, the narcissist showers their partner with excessive attention, affection, and praise. This behaviour is often referred to as "love bombing."

The narcissist presents an idealised version of themselves, mirroring their partner's interests and desires. They may make grand

SIX THINGS NARCISSISTS DO BEHIND YOUR BACK

1. Smear your name to gain sympathy and control.
2. Pretend to be the victim in your story.
3. Tell half-truths or twisted versions of events.
4. Flirt or seek attention from others for validation.
5. Undermine your credibility with friends or family.
6. Study your weaknesses to use them against you later.

MENTAL HEALTH

romantic gestures or promise a perfect future together. This creates an intense emotional connection and feelings of euphoria in their partner.

The idealisation phase can last anywhere from a few weeks to several months. During this time, the narcissist gathers information about their partner's vulnerabilities and desires, which they later use for manipulation.

Devaluation Phase

As the relationship progresses, the narcissist begins to show their true colours. The devaluation phase is characterised by increasing criticism, emotional manipulation, and withdrawal of affection.

The narcissist may: • Belittle their partner's achievements • Make hurtful comments disguised as jokes • Compare their partner unfavourably to others • Withhold affection as punishment.

Gaslighting becomes common during this stage. The narcissist denies or distorts reality, making their partner question their own perceptions and memories. This erodes the partner's self-esteem and confidence.

The devaluation phase can last for months or even years. The narcissist alternates between moments of charm and cruelty, keeping their partner off-balance and hoping for a return to the idealisation phase.

Discard Phase

In the discard phase, the narcissist rejects their partner, often in a cruel or abrupt manner. This may involve:

• Sudden abandonment
• Initiating a breakup
• Cheating or starting a new relationship
• Emotional withdrawal while maintaining the relationship in name only

The discard phase can be devastating for the partner, who may have invested significant emotional energy into the relationship. The narcissist often blames their partner for the relationship's failure, further damaging their self-esteem.

It's important to note that the discard may not be permanent. Narcissists often return to previous partners for attention or resources, restarting the cycle with renewed idealisation.

The Consequences of Long-Term Abuse

Prolonged narcissistic abuse can lead to severe psychological effects. Victims may develop complex post-traumatic stress disorder (CPTSD) due to ongoing trauma. Symptoms include hypervigilance, emotional flashbacks, disassociation and difficulty with self-regulation.

Trauma bonding often occurs, causing victims to feel attached to their abusers despite the harm. This bond can make it challenging to leave the relationship. Survivors may struggle with self-esteem issues and have difficulty trusting others.

Recovery requires professional support and time to heal. Therapy can help victims process their experiences and develop healthy coping mechanisms.

Building a support network is crucial for long-term healing and breaking the cycle of abuse.

Recovering from narcissistic abuse requires implementing effective strategies and seeking support. Establishing boundaries, focusing on healing, and moving forward are crucial steps in the recovery process.

Establishing and Maintaining Boundaries

Setting clear boundaries is essential for recovery from narcissistic abuse. Victims should limit contact with the narcissist and enforce consequences for boundary violations. The "grey rock" technique can be useful, involving minimal emotional responses to the narcissist's provocations.

Boundaries extend to digital spaces as well. Blocking the narcissist on social media and restricting their access to personal information helps maintain emotional distance.

It's important to communicate boundaries firmly and consistently. This may involve enlisting the support of trusted friends or family members to help enforce these limits.

Strategies for Healing

Healing from narcissistic abuse often involves addressing **C-PTSD symptoms**.

Seeking therapy from mental health professionals experienced in narcissistic abuse recovery is crucial.

Self-care practices are vital:

- ♥ Regular exercise
- ♥ Meditation or mindfulness
- ♥ Journaling
- ♥ Engaging in hobbies
- ♥ Building self-esteem is a key aspect of healing. This can involve:
- ♥ Positive self-talk
- ♥ Setting and achieving small goals
- ♥ Recognising personal strengths
- ♥ Support groups provide a safe space to share experiences and learn coping strategies from others who have faced similar challenges.
- ♥ Moving Forward After Narcissistic Abuse
- ♥ Moving forward involves rebuilding a life free from narcissistic influence. This process may include:
- ♥ Rediscovering personal interests and passions
- ♥ Forming new, healthy relationships
- ♥ Setting and pursuing personal goals

Closure is often an important step. This may not involve direct confrontation with the narcissist, but rather internal acceptance and letting go.

Developing a strong support network is crucial. This can include trusted friends, family members, and mental health professionals who understand the impact of narcissistic abuse.

It's important to be patient with the recovery process. Healing takes time, and setbacks are normal. Celebrating small victories along the way can boost motivation and reinforce progress.

https://www.ourmental.health/narcissists/essential-narcissist-terms-understanding-the-language-of-narcissistic-behavior

> AFTER A WHILE I LOOKED IN THE MIRROR AND REALIZED...WOW AFTER ALL THOSE HURTS, SCARS, AND BRUISES, AFTER ALL OF THOSE TRIALS, I REALLY MADE IT THROUGH. I DID IT. I SURVIVED THAT WHICH WAS SUPPOSED TO KILL ME. SO I STRAIGHTENED MY CROWN...AND WALKED AWAY LIKE A BOSS.

www.ingramcontent.com/pod-product-compliance
Lightning Source LLC
Chambersburg PA
CBHW031156020426
42333CB00013B/693